FIGHT THROUGH CARTOONS

FIGHT THROUGH CARTOONS

My story of harassment, intimidation & jail

ZUNAR

Assisted by SUKHBIR CHEEMA

© 2019 Marshall Cavendish International (Asia) Private Limited
Text and illustrations © Zunar

Reprinted 2019

Published by Marshall Cavendish Editions
An imprint of Marshall Cavendish International

All rights reserved

No part of this publication may be reproduced, stored in a retrieval system or transmitted, in any form or by any means, electronic, mechanical, photocopying, recording or otherwise, without the prior permission of the copyright owner. Requests for permission should be addressed to the Publisher, Marshall Cavendish International (Asia) Private Limited, 1 New Industrial Road, Singapore 536196. Tel: (65) 6213 9300.
Email: genref@sg.marshallcavendish.com
Website: www.marshallcavendish.com/genref

The publisher makes no representation or warranties with respect to the contents of this book, and specifically disclaims any implied warranties or merchantability or fitness for any particular purpose, and shall in no event be liable for any loss of profit or any other commercial damage, including but not limited to special, incidental, consequential, or other damages.

Other Marshall Cavendish Offices:
Marshall Cavendish Corporation, 99 White Plains Road, Tarrytown NY 10591-9001, USA • Marshall Cavendish International (Thailand) Co Ltd, 253 Asoke, 12th Flr, Sukhumvit 21 Road, Klongtoey Nua, Wattana, Bangkok 10110, Thailand • Marshall Cavendish (Malaysia) Sdn Bhd, Times Subang, Lot 46, Subang Hi-Tech Industrial Park, Batu Tiga, 40000 Shah Alam, Selangor Darul Ehsan, Malaysia.

Marshall Cavendish is a registered trademark of Times Publishing Limited

National Library Board, Singapore Cataloguing in Publication Data

Names: Zunar.
Title: Fight through cartoons : my story of harassment, intimidation & jail / Zunar.
Description: Singapore : Marshall Cavendish Editions, [2019]
Identifiers: OCN 1091060593 | 978-981-48-4122-1 (paperback)
Subjects: LCSH: Zunar. | Cartoonists--Malaysia--Biography. | Malaysia--Politics and government--21st century--Caricatures and cartoons.
Classification: DDC 320.9595--dc23

Printed in Singapore

Cover photo by Sukhbir Cheema. Assisted by Azman MatNoh.

To ,

"Kartini"

CONTENTS

FOREWORD — 9
Truth over Tyranny

AN INTRODUCTION TO MALAYSIAN POLITICS — 15

CHAPTER 1 — 23
Power of the Pen
Method of drawing cartoons

CHAPTER 2 — 39
They Cannot Ban My Mind
The story of *Gedung Kartun*

CHAPTER 3 — 53
Pinch or Punch?
Perak Darul Kartun

CHAPTER 4 — 61
Even My Pen has a Stand
1 Funny Malaysia and *Isu Dalam Kartun*

CHAPTER 5 — 74
My Cartoons are Dangerous!
Battle at the courts

CHAPTER 6 — 82
Cartoon-O-Phobia
Sedition and handcuffs

CHAPTER 7 — 102
Arrest of the Assistants
Pirates of the Carry-BN and *The Conspiracy to Imprison Anwar*

CHAPTER 8   117
Talent is Not a Gift
Of Birkin, rings and diamonds

CHAPTER 9   129
"Scratch and Win" the Law
Funny and spicy cartoons

CHAPTER 10   137
Twit, Twit
Nights in police lock-up

CHAPTER 11   154
Which is Bigger, Fear or Responsibility?
Nine sedition charges, 43 years' jail

CHAPTER 12   172
Prisoner in Homeland
Meeting Kofi Annan in Geneva

CHAPTER 13   189
Me Against Gangsters
Cartoon exhibition attacked and smashed

CHAPTER 14   211
The Illegal Tea
Detrimental to parliamentary democracy

CHAPTER 15   226
Struggle is an Endless Marathon
If you cannot beat them, laugh at them

EPILOGUE   248

ABOUT THE AUTHOR   255

TRUTH OVER TYRANNY

Zunar's *Fight Through Cartoons* is not so much about a world-famous cartoonist and the cartoons that have played such a role in changing the history of his country of Malaysia as it is a journey through pain, bravery, risk-taking, and, we hope (because his story is far from over), a final victory for courage and Zunar's breed of truth over tyranny.

His book is important to the history of the battle for human rights. It is not the typical inventory of political cartoons about a certain topic or over a particular political period. Zunar has given us what is quite rare in the world of human rights and political cartooning. He opens the door into the anatomy of how a tyrant and demagogue uses the tools and institutions of state power to stop the critics that would point the world's attention to their lawlessness, tyranny and demagoguery.

The best political cartoonists are a breed apart. They land somewhere in between Don Quixote tilting at windmills, and

Gandhi making salt under the noses of the British. Very serious stuff that we are expected to laugh at: Samuel Clemens once wrote, "Against the assault of laughter nothing can stand." Confirming this, 25 years ago one of the first lessons I learned, as a human rights worker focusing on political cartoonists in trouble, was that tyrants can usually survive any challenge except that of their people laughing at them. Rebels can be defeated by the army with a couple of tanks. International human rights organizations can be deconstructed into powerless paper tigers. Your nation's resources can be sold to powerful international corporate interests who will protect the tyrant and thereby protect their investors. Laughing at tyrants can have some strange results. One of our clients reported that a man in a small town picked up a newspaper off the street, turned to the political cartoon and started laughing hysterically. A passing policeman arrested him and charged him with insulting the head of state. Not the cartoonist: the reader who laughed.

What is so important about Zunar's *Fight Through Cartoons* is how he gives historians, human rights students and workers, political cartoonists, free-speech advocates, and freedom of speech researchers an insider's personal roadmap on how a tyrannical government shuts down free speech. This one man's intimate roadmap about his own personal journey is relatively difficult to find in the literature surrounding freedom of speech and human rights.

No action takes place in isolation. Everything is context. For the tyrants of the world to be countered by mere mortals, the world of the tyrant and the tyrants' reach must be understood in great depth. The modern democracies, and the large and hopefully powerful nongovernmental organizations whose missions charge them to fight the tyrants, all must operate under policies, management procedures, chains of command, competing interests with other organizations, considerations about their funding sources, that put limitations on their actions. The well entrenched tyrant is not bothered by any considerations of the democratic process. Once the tyrant has gained control over the legislative bodies, the police and crime investigators, the judicial system right up to the Supreme Court and, of course, the media, the tyrant pays little attention to traditional rules or regulations of democratic governance. They are free to constantly and immediately evolve strategies and methods to crush those who challenge them. Bilateral and multilateral agencies like the UN must adhere to all the above bureaucratic challenges when changing policies or taking new directions to counteract the dance of the tyrants. Any good self-respecting tyrant can run circles around the administratively restricted governments and agencies working against him or her.

Zunar is showing us how he used the tyrant's own systems created to work against him to work for him. How very clever and, in so doing, he challenges the status quo of the human rights advocacy world to confront their own inability to respond quickly to the ever-changing new strategies and methods of the tyrant. In his book, *Fight Through Cartoons*, we see Zunar in the ring with a George Foreman, and he's just dancing around, fluttering like a butterfly and stinging like a bee.

In the world of editorial cartoonists, we like to think that a good political cartoon makes you think. For me, that doesn't do it. If the cartoonist doesn't make me feel, then the job isn't complete. It might be the difference between the very best cartoons motivating readers to write a letter of complaint to a congressperson or local politician, but when you are made to feel, you join a movement in protest in the streets.

Zunar's now infamous cartoon of him in chains, handcuffs and ropes straining with his pen in his mouth to complete a drawing is such a cartoon. The cartoon was drawn during one of his darkest days when he was facing continued arrests, harassment, possibly years in prison, and when the Najib government seemed to be at the peak of its power – this  was the time that he produced the most emotionally powerful cartoon of his life. This cartoon helped galvanize and focus the entire human rights and cartooning world to feel what it's like to have their lives stripped, their character dirtied, their honor compromised, and their whole family terrorized. Anyone who has ever had the proverbial rug pulled out from underneath them and left to dangle alone in the cold or who has been shunned by their community will feel exactly what Zunar has felt.

I will also say that in my 25 years of experience with Cartoonist Rights Network International and the dozens upon dozens of cartoonists I and our Board of Directors and staff have worked with over the years, that post-traumatic stress disorder at some level or another is the most common short and long impact that a cartoonist under extreme threat can feel. Their ability to plan, their inability to see their situation clearly and objectively, the slow but inexorable withdrawal of friends and even family, the institutions of power that should be protecting now used against you, it all leaves the cartoonist with a profound sense of isolation and helplessness. It seems that there is no one there to help you. No one understands what you have experienced. Things are going on in your head and in your life that you dare not speak about. While to my knowledge none of our cartoonists have committed suicide, many of them are left broken, strangers in strange lands, with no guidelines on how to climb out, and persevere and survive.

Most, like Zunar, have shown incredible moral resilience and a willingness to dare to hope and continue fighting under any circumstances.

A few years ago, when Zunar and I were having breakfast over our kitchen table in my home, I asked him bluntly, "Zunar, why don't you just leave the country, seek a foreign safe haven home, and put all of this behind you?" He looked at me as if I were speaking another language. Despite being one of the most even-tempered people I've ever met, he almost got up out of his chair and said, "Who the hell are these people to think that this is their country? This is my country, this is our country, why should I even consider leaving it. No, I stay and fight. They leave."

This is the call that Zunar has made: tell the truth, fight tyranny. His wife is just as brave as he is, and luckily for them, in the last national election in Malaysia, the old corrupt government has been replaced. Zunar's decade-long fight is over for now. Of course, until the new regime finds that the taste of money is sweet, and when you're at the top of the heap, the stuff is all around you.

Dr Robert Russell
Executive Director
Cartoonists Rights Network International

For over 60 years since Malaysia's independence on August 31, 1957, the country has been ruled by Barisan Nasional, a coalition consisting of race-based parties such as the United Malays National Organisation (Umno), the Malaysian Chinese Association (MCA) and the Malaysian Indian Congress (MIC). While the coalition's founding fathers will always be remembered for the role they played in the country's independence, the recent generation of leaders have only led the coalition to disgrace.

Yet the coalition stayed strong in power because many of Malaysia's older generation who lived through the independence era had grown comfortable with and accustomed to Barisan Nasional, which had played a pivotal role in granting the nation independence from the British. By the 1980s, despite the political persecutions by Mahathir Mohamad, many Malaysians felt that they

should not rock the boat because the country was doing well economically under Mahathir. It was during Mahathir's first tenure as prime minister when oppressive archaic law such as the Internal Security Act was used to silence critics. It was also during this period that Barisan Nasional gradually grew even more corrupt through the practice of cronyism.

The first cracks in the coalition became visible in 1998 when Mahathir sacked his deputy, Anwar Ibrahim, and subsequently jailed him on trumped-up sodomy charges. Mahathir had set the wheels in motion for the gradual demise of the world's oldest ruling government and the eventual first democratic change of power in Malaysia.

The late 1990s was marked the era of Reformasi (Reformation). Malaysians gradually awoke to the type of government that they were dealing with. Among them was Zunar, who had taken a sabbatical from cartooning. The events of that year brought him to his senses and he decided to use cartoons as a platform to voice his feelings and thoughts about his country.

By the time Anwar was released from prison in 2004, Mahathir was succeeded by Abdullah Ahmad Badawi. Anwar rose to the limelight again, this time as a charismatic opposition leader who united his party, the Parti

Keadilan Rakyat (PKR), together with other opposition parties such as the Democratic Action Party (DAP) and the Parti Islam Se-Malaysia (PAS), to form Malaysia's strongest opposition coalition, Pakatan Rakyat (People's Coalition).

During the 12th general election on March 8, 2008, Pakatan Rakyat dealt a blow to Barisan Nasional. For the first time since 1969, the ruling government no longer held two-thirds' majority in the Malaysian parliament.

Abdullah Badawi stepped down a year after the elections and was succeeded by his deputy, the scandal riddled Najib Razak, on April 3, 2009.

This period marked a dark time for Malaysia: under Najib's tenure, corruption was at its peak. This snowballed to a rise in the cost of living. Coupled with that were several high-profile scandals under Najib's belt, such as the murder of Mongolian model Altantuyaa Shaariibuu, the Scorpene submarine scandal and brazen corruption in the form of the 1Malaysia Development Berhad (1MDB) scandal.

Under Najib's rule, the media was controlled heavily, the police no longer protected the innocent and the judiciary was no longer as trustworthy as it used to be. Prominent critics of Najib's government were harassed and intimidated. Zunar had thousands of his books seized, nearly all of his titles banned, his printers threatened, his assistants arrested by the police, and he was punched, jailed and banned from travelling. The list of tactics the government utilised to silence the cartoonist was exhaustive.

In Malaysian newspapers, Zunar's cartoons were not found. Media organisations were not allowed to publish his cartoons as they were deemed controversial and seditious. Anything that painted Najib's government in a negative light was omitted from the papers. Several major dailies were also biased in their reporting. The only media organisation which was bold enough to showcase his cartoons was 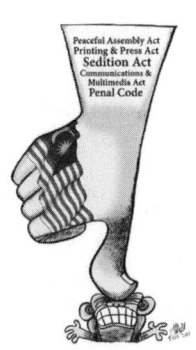 Malaysia's first independent news portal, Malaysiakini, which was free from the government's influence. They, too, were harassed by Najib's government and were threatened into silence.

Yet, despite the odds stacked against him, Zunar continued to punch his way through cartoons, utilising out-of-the-box tactics, which were not only humorous but effective as well.

In the process of writing this book, Zunar has remarked that his struggle against the Barisan Nasional regime was akin to a chess game. There were times when he was a step ahead of his opponent and there were moments when they were ahead.

 Politics, however, is more than a chess game to Zunar. It is a game that can seal the fate of the country and determine the lives of millions of Malaysians. At the political forefront, Najib could not be removed easily as he continued staying in power after the 13th general election in 2013. His second term as prime minister was worse than the first as more news about Barisan Nasional's mismanagement of the nation surfaced, thanks to the Internet.

During this period, opposition leader Anwar was sentenced to prison, again, in 2015. It was a blatant attempt at political assassination to silence one of the strongest proponents of change in Malaysia. Najib was preparing to woo the voters and continue to stay on in power. With Anwar out of the coming election, Najib had an open path towards his electoral victory.

Following the 13th general election, he immediately started on a silencing spree, targeting all of his critics in what is now dubbed Operasi Lalang II (Operation Lalang II). While domestically many activists, lawyers, opposition lawmakers, journalists, academics and cartoonists such as Zunar were thrown behind bars and charged under the colonial era Sedition Act, internationally, Malaysia became a laughing stock.

The morale of the nation plummeted as Najib began tightening his grip on power, unperturbed by the 1MDB scandal which broke out in 2015. Zunar was charged under the Sedition Act for nine counts of criticising  the government on Twitter and satirising Najib, his wife, Rosmah Mansor, and lawmakers from Barisan Nasional. Just for drawing cartoons that criticised the ruling government, Zunar found himself staring at 43 years in jail.

However, censorship was not new to Zunar. When he was 18, a cartoon he had drawn for a school magazine was blackened. In Malaysia, a culture of self-censorship has been prevalent and instilled in the minds of children at a young age under Barisan Nasional's rule. It was one of the methods employed to keep Malaysians dumbed down through education.

By 2016, issues of race and religion began surfacing again with several incidences that tried to test the united strength of the Malaysian people. PAS broke off from Pakatan Rakyat and began getting cosier with Umno. All hope was lost.

Online, cartoonists such as Zunar began doubling their efforts to educate the public through social media on how politics played a role in the lives of the common people and stressed the importance of casting aside racial and religious differences to get together to boot out a corrupt and tyrannical government.

Utilising various social media platforms such as Twitter, Facebook, Instagram and YouTube to reach out to as many Malaysians as possible, Zunar gave many the courage to laugh at the oppressors through his cartoons.

As Malaysia descended into a state of hopelessness by late 2016, through a political twist, Mahathir re-entered the political fray and joined hands with his former nemesis turned ally, Anwar, to form Pakatan Harapan (Coalition of Hope) in an effort to end Najib's misrule and Barisan Nasional's mismanagement of Malaysia.

On May 9, 2018, at the historic 14th general election, Malaysia won a new government for herself.

While on television and in the newspapers these two names were mentioned frequently in the same breath, the true change was actually made possible thanks to the Malaysian people. Behind it all were the many activists and cartoonists such as Zunar, who played a pivotal role in bringing about the end of Barisan Nasional's 60 years in power.

This book chronicles Zunar's fight through cartoons from 2009 to 2018. Peppered within the pages of this book are some of Zunar's timeless philosophies on cartooning, which kept him going despite the odds stacked against him. These philosophies, if reflected on and internalised, could inspire anyone who wishes to fight injustice through the arts.

In this book, Zunar also sheds light on the methodological approach he utilises in his cartoons to effectively deliver his messages. From the conception of a cartoon right down to inking it, Zunar bares what goes on his mind when he draws his cartoons.

From being labelled controversial to becoming an award-winning cartoonist, this is Zunar's fight through cartoons in his own words.

Sukhbir Cheema
Writer, Cartoonist & Co-Founder of Eksentrika

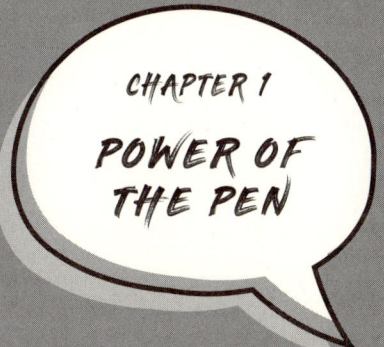

POWER OF THE PEN
Method of drawing cartoons

LOOKING BACK ON MY SCHOOL DAYS, drawing cartoons was just a hobby for me. Initially, I wanted to be a scientist, but along the way, my life took a different path. Now, I have ended up with a studio full of pens, pencils, brushes, ink and paper.

I don't draw what I see. I draw what I think. Some cartoonists have to go out to get inspired, but I don't travel. I only travel for events and exhibitions. For my cartoons, I travel in my mind. The way I draw cartoons is different from other cartoonists. Speaking about talent, however, I have to admit that technically, I'm not as good as some cartoonists in terms of strokes and artistic touch.

However, I believe that technical skill is not the only quality required in drawing political cartoons. I would say that good political cartoons should consist of 50% technique and 50% subject matter. Or it could be 30% technique and 70% about the subject. That is why, for me, the information, the stand and the direction are very important in my work. The process is usually like this: I start off by researching the issue in question. I research about issues from different perspectives and do not limit myself to only a few sources. The Internet has made me more resourceful.

Sometimes, some of these issues are related to people I know personally, so I would call them to get more details on the matter, as news can sometimes be misreported and become inaccurate.

Through this detailed and thorough research, I am able to defend my cartoons when they come under legal or political attack. After the research process, I take a stand on the issue and lock it in.

Next in my process would be the direction of the cartoon. This basically means how I want people to react when they see my cartoons. What do I expect my readers' reaction to be? I make sure that my cartoons have a very clear direction.

The last step is when the joke comes in. At this point, I have not started drawing yet. All of these are still in my mind and it can take six to seven hours before I finally turn them into visual images on paper.

For me, it is important that the jokes must be in line with my earlier three steps. A joke must support my research, my stand and the direction of the cartoon.

If the joke is not in line with my stand and the available facts, I will not use it.

Only when I get the joke will I begin drawing the concept for the cartoon. I will not draw directly on drawing paper but I will do a very rough sketch of the concept on a small piece of paper or any scrap of paper which I find on my table.

During the concept stage, I decide on the size of the object I am drawing in order to make it more impactful in highlighting the issue.

This is why on one day I may draw character A bigger than character B, and on other days, character B may be bigger than character A. The same goes for other objects such as a ring, a Birkin bag or a money bag.

In terms of presentation, I also need to decide if a cartoon should be drawn in one, two or more panels.

Whatever I draw, it must support the message to be conveyed. Sometimes, I am about to finish a drawing when I realise that the drawing overshadows the message. When this happens, I would adjust or even redraw the cartoon in order to make the message visually captivating.

This step can vary from one cartoon to the next.

My aim is to draw cartoons which explore issues at a deeper level and not just remain on the surface of issues. I believe that when a cartoonist goes deeper into an issue, he or she will gain a better understanding about it.

I don't want my readers to just laugh, I want them to get emotional. This is why I go deep into an issue. The analogy is as follows: if I stand on a beach, I can see the ocean with so many beautiful things on the surface, but that is not good enough for my cartoon; I have to dive deep into the ocean and see things from that perspective. Through this process will I know what is inside the hearts of the people and draw a cartoon that reflects their emotions and sentiments. The art that comes from hands, reaches eyes, but the art that comes from the heart, reaches hearts. It is challenging, but I am happy doing it this way, my way.

After I'm satisfied with the visual concept, I then start to sketch using a pencil on drawing paper. I have A3-sized special drawing paper that I feel comfortable with. After penciling, I use pen and brush to ink my cartoons in black and white. After all is completed, I scan it to my laptop and use Photoshop to colour it.

On inking my cartoons, the chosen colours play an important role, too. I select colours which make my cartoons impactful. From the concept to colouring, the entire process can take up to three or four hours.

To draw a cartoon, or (my preferred word) to "compose" a cartoon, takes me up to 12 hours.

I believe a simple cartoon is more effective for the people. Sometimes, you just need one object to represent all the issues. Sometimes, you need very little words as well.

I make sure to use simple words. I have English and Malay readers who read my cartoons, so I use words which can be understood by both groups. For example, the word "sapu", which means "steal" in Malay, is understood by everyone in Malaysia.

Visually, my cartoons are very minimal. I don't draw backgrounds and leave it as simple as possible. This is because the issues in my cartoons are very heavy, so I want people to have a clear mind to read and focus on the message that I want to convey to them.

In terms of using words, I also change them depending on the issues at the time. In my early cartoons, I used a lot of English words but, later on, I began using more Malay words, too. This is because I think English readers, who are normally from a middle-class background, already have a knowledge about the issues in the country, but by using more Malay words, I can engage more people on the street and those in the rural areas. In the more recent cartoons, I try to minimise the use of words and concentrate more on visuals.

I usually work in the mornings, when my mind is fresh. This is when the ideas I get are solid because my mind is more energetic. I sometimes even wake up at 5am to draw.

The other reason why mornings are very important to me is because my cartoons should be uploaded early in the morning. This is the time when traffic in social media is at its peak, when people have taken their breakfast and before they go to work — it is the best time to reach maximum readers. Since my cartoons can only be published on the Internet and through social media, this is a very important approach and process for my cartoons.

A sample of my doodles which nobody understands, including myself, with the passage of time.

Below and on the following pages are some of my iconic cartoons.

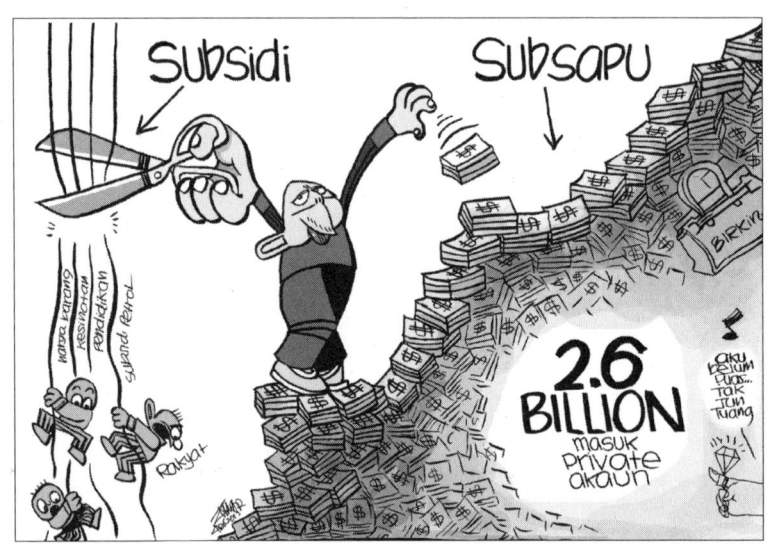
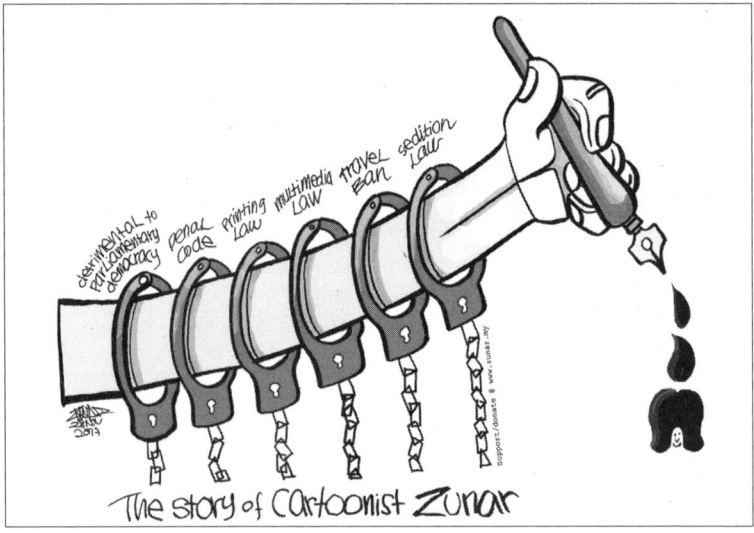

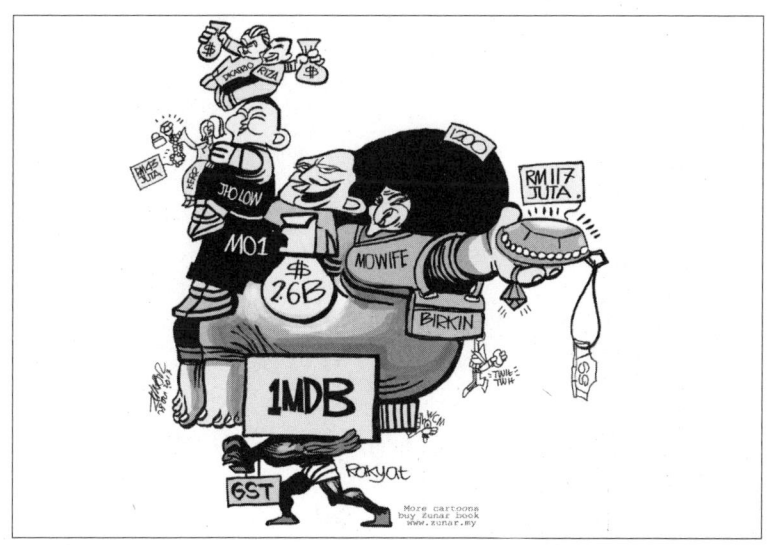

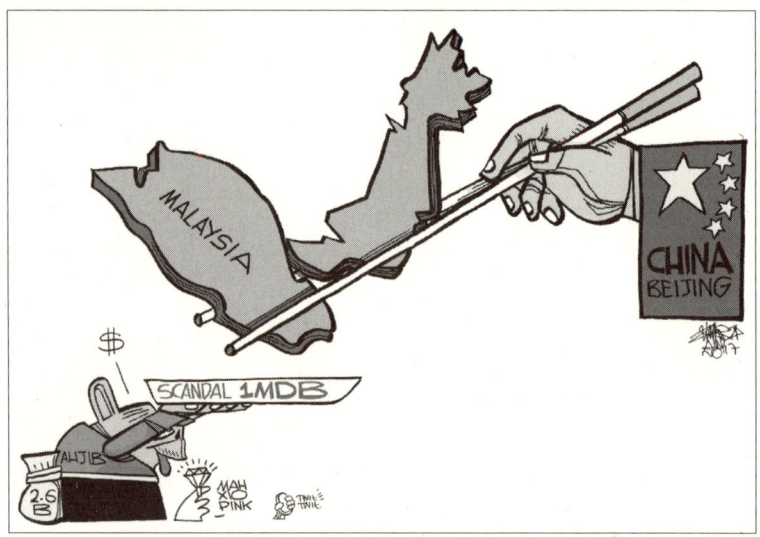

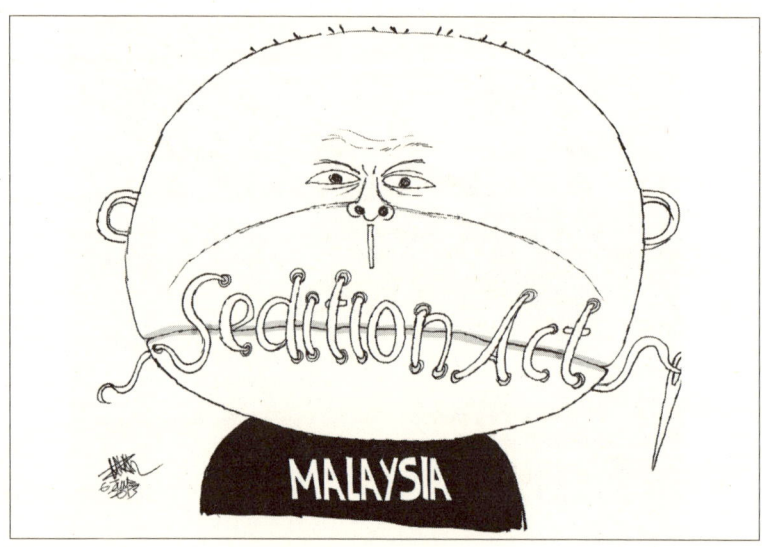

CHAPTER 2
THEY CANNOT BAN MY MIND

THEY CANNOT BAN MY MIND
The story of *Gedung Kartun*

I HAVE ALWAYS ENJOYED DRAWING cartoons from as early as I can remember, but I did not have any formal education in art or cartooning. This was due to my late parents, SM Anwarul Haque and Khadizah Mohamad, wanting me to study science because, for them, it was an area which held a very bright future for me. I was sent to a science stream school, but this did not stop me from drawing cartoons. I started very early, but I am not able to recall the age when I started to draw. My first cartoon was published by a children's magazine called *Bambino* when I was 12 years old. After that, I kept sending more cartoons to the publisher and once in a while they would get published. I did not get any payment but would receive a free copy with a thank-you note stamped on it. This was a priceless gift for me at that time and I used to show it to every friend in my village; it was special because others had to buy the magazine while I had a complimentary copy.

As time passed, I started to develop the idea of including some sort of message in my cartoons. I think this is the best way of cartooning, even though it is not in the Malaysian culture to do so. Not surprisingly, my first controversy came when I was 17 years old and in Form 5: I was reprimanded for drawing a cartoon in the school's magazine that criticised the teachers. This was the moment when I began to view things critically. Later in my career, in my early 30s, the same thing happened when I worked for a newspaper called *Berita Harian*.

I went to university to take a science course as I had obtained good results in chemistry and biology. In the first year of university, I faced a dilemma of whether to choose art or science. I went to the university's administrator to change my course to architecture, but I was not successful because I did not have any qualifications in the arts. I started to lose interest in science and did not take the first-year examination. Finally, I dropped out from the course and university. I did not tell my parents for six months. They thought I was still in university while I stayed in Kuala Lumpur and worked as a construction labourer and cleaner, and took several jobs as a factory worker until I got an offer to work in a government hospital.

While I had a steady job at the hospital, I continued to draw cartoons. My career as a cartoonist progressed very well. By then, I already had a permanent column in a magazine called *Gila Gila*. During the day, I did laboratory work analysing lab test results and in the night, I drew cartoons. When I had more columns to fill, I faced the question of whether to become a full-time cartoonist or work in the field of science. The government job was secure with a stable future, but working as a cartoonist was not. This dilemma went on for some time until I started to lose my mathematical skills because I was focusing more on drawing. As a result, I started to make mistakes in my laboratory test reports. I was constantly scolded by my superior because the mistakes I made were life threatening to the patients. I then resigned and became a freelance cartoonist with various magazines and newspapers.

In general, the cartooning industry in Malaysia was booming with the rise of many professional cartoonists and publications. However, I was still not able to convey messages in my cartoons because of the strict censorship by the editors of the magazines and newspapers.

Still, there was something missing in the cartooning scene in Malaysia. We had many cartoonists drawing for newspapers and magazines, but the content of the cartoons lacked any political message and criticism. Even when there was such content, it was usually in the form of propaganda for the government.

This was strange, because we had so many issues of corruption and abuse of power around us, such as the murder of the Mongolian model, Altantuya Shaariibuu, and the Scorpene submarine scandal. There were just no cartoons on these issues of the day.

While I was contributing daily political cartoons for Malaysiakini, which focused on fighting corruption and abuse of power, I felt there was a need to gather a group of cartoonists to produce satirical works as a team. I started to plan a political cartoon magazine. I wanted the magazine to be really punchy and impactful, unlike those already available in the market.

My vision was to make readers aware of what was happening at that time. I felt it was important to use cartoons as a tool of information and education in society. I noticed there were several fresh, independent cartoonists who shared their cartoons on social media, such as Jonos, Haili, Johnny Ong, Ronasina and others. So I called them and few others to discuss my idea. We finally agreed to come out with a cartoon magazine titled *Gedung Kartun* (Cartoon Store).

We gathered some capital from donors and the public to obtain an office that included a studio in Brickfields, Kuala Lumpur. We set up a company called Sepakat Efektif in May 2009, with 12 staff members, including cartoonists, editors, graphic artists, administrators and marketing personnel. They were editor Fandiramli, chief cartoonist Jonos, who had cartoonists under him such as Ronasina, Roy, Cabai, Madsein, Kidol, Haili, Enot, Kawe, Oly, Abdullah Jones, Deng, Ubilepih, Nur, Dikuk and Fahmi — and myself as the chief editor.

Nazruddin Abu Bakar and Munirah Yasin helped me with the magazine's graphics and multimedia was under Syafiq Sunny. On the management side, Jasmine Ng served as the administrative head, Azzam Supardi as the production manager, Israq Ismail was in charge of the magazine's distribution, while Maisuri Zainal took care of the management of the company. The magazine was to be printed by K Vin Publisher.

We submitted a licence application, together with a mock-up of the magazine, to the Home Ministry (KDN) for approval. The approval by the ministry was compulsory. To give *Gedung Kartun* more bite, I contacted respectable national laureate, A. Samad Said, to contribute his writings, and I was extraordinarily pleased when he agreed as he was (and is) such a big name with a large following in Malaysia. In addition, the other famous writer and poet, Pyanhabib, had also agreed to contribute to *Gedung Kartun*.

We started the groundwork with meetings, discussions and brainstorming sessions to come up with the full idea and concept of the magazine. We agreed it would be 100% satire from the front to the back cover, be it in the form of cartoons, illustrations, comics or writings. The magazine focused on the four big political issues at that time.

First, the Scorpene scandal and the murder of Altantuya. These were in reference to the purchase of two submarines from a French company in 2002 when Prime Minister Najib Razak was Defence Minister. It was reported by foreign media that there was a million-dollar kickback. During the negotiations in Paris, Altantuya, who was said to be very close to Najib, was present. Altantuya was killed in 2006 in Malaysia and those who were arrested were close associates of Najib.

Second, the death of opposition political aide, Teoh Beng Hock, who was found dead at the Malaysian Anti-Corruption Commission (MACC) building after he was investigated by the commission. The third major issue was the imprisonment of the charismatic and popular opposition leader, Anwar Ibrahim. The fourth issue was the lavish spending of the prime minister's wife, Rosmah Mansor, and the misuse of power by Najib's administration.

While waiting for the approval from KDN, everybody started to work towards the deadline. Along the way, there were many other cartoonists who sent in their cartoons as contributors. Several weeks later, my marketing staff informed me that we had received a serial number from KDN as initial approval for the licence. This was good news and things looked smooth.

The big day finally arrived on August 23, 2009 when the first batch of *Gedung Kartun* was delivered to my office. I was relieved and excited because all the hard work was paying off. More importantly, my dream of having my type of cartooning published was finally becoming a reality. All of the creative and management staff were happy because their months of sweat and effort were paying off. The new era of cartooning had begun. This was the one and only satirical cartoon magazine in Malaysia that dared to criticise with its strong, punchy and provocative messages.

The magazine was distributed to bookstores nationwide and it sold for RM5. It was a very low price because I wanted more Malaysians, especially in the rural areas, to be able to afford the magazine. The precedent had been set up and I thought it would be followed by others. To show my appreciation and happiness, I hosted a small *buka puasa* (breaking fast) ceremony for the staff and all those who were involved in the magazine.

While having the meal, I spoke about a plan to launch this magazine officially and to invite some politicians to launch it. A few names were suggested but one of the writers, Pyanhabib, suggested that I should invite Home Ministry officers to launch *Gedung Kartun*. I laughed and said it was a funny idea but did not take it seriously. Everybody laughed as well.

On August 25, 2009, two days after the publication, I was at my office with my staff, planning the materials for the second issue of *Gedung Kartun*. My clerk, Maisuri, suddenly rushed into my room with a panicked look on her face. She told me there were six suspicious but smart-looking people in coat and tie at the door who wanted to see to me. I asked her who they were, but she said she didn't know. So I went out to the front door to find out for myself.

The group of people introduced themselves as officers from the Home Ministry's Publications Control and Al-Quran Text Division. I asked them to come in and take a seat. At that moment, I suddenly remembered the joke about having Home Ministry officers launch *Gedung Kartun*. I felt that something was not right and I asked them what the matter was. The head of the team told me that she had received a report that I had published an illegal magazine without a licence (permit) from the Home Ministry. Obviously, she was referring to *Gedung Kartun*. As a result of this, she said she wanted to confiscate the magazines. I told her it was not true as I had applied for the permit and had official verbal approval, and that it would only take some time to receive the official documents. I picked up a copy and showed them the serial number at the top of the cover, but they said the serial number was not official.

After a heated shouting exchange, I finally had to back down and they began to seize the magazines. It was unfortunate that I had 408 copies of *Gedung Kartun* at the lobby area of my office that were supposed to be distributed later. I asked for a warrant but they said that under the Printing Presses and Publication Act (PPPA), they did not need a warrant to confiscate "illegal magazines". I had no choice but to let them take all the magazines. However, since I could not do anything to stop them, I decided to make it difficult for them by creating a big issue out of it. I made them count and recount, and put on proper record the copies that were to be taken. I did this to buy time.

While the officers busied themselves counting the magazines, I secretly contacted a journalist from alternative web-portal Malaysiakini to come over, but my contact told me it would take him around half an hour to arrive, so I had to buy more time. After the counting had finished, the officer informed me that the total number of magazines was 408. I said I was not satisfied because the number should be more than that, and I asked for a recount. This was a tactic to ensure the journalist would arrive before the officers left my office.

The tactic paid off because the journalist arrived before the second recount was completed. All the magazines were taken and I couldn't do anything to stop them, but before they stepped out of my office, the news was already circulating on the Internet. The headline,

"KDN serbu pejabat Zunar" (Home Ministry raids Zunar's office), went viral online. The reaction from the public was sarcastic and cynical. Many slammed the government for harassing a cartoonist.

I suspect the raid was not because of the licence, but what was on the cover of *Gedung Kartun*. The cover depicted Prime Minister Najib Razak holding a flag to celebrate Malaysia's independence day and shouting, "Merdeka!" (Freedom!) The cartoon also shows him holding a Mongolian flag and a small character pulling on his trousers and saying, "You got it wrong, Sir. That is not a Malaysian flag, it's a Mongolian flag." The cartoon made fun of the issue of the murder of the Mongolian model, Altantuya. The public believed that this was somehow connected to the prime minister because the suspects arrested were his advisor and bodyguard. This issue was considered taboo and a very sensitive topic in Malaysia. No mainstream media dared to publish an opinion or make big news out of it.

The next day, Home Ministry officers raided the printer, K Vin Publisher, in Seri Kembangan, Selangor. They confiscated printing plates and warned the printer that their whole business licence would be revoked if they continued to print my books and magazines. For the record, the printing licence falls under the jurisdiction of the PPPA. In Malaysia, not only publishers but also printers have to renew their licence every year according to the law. So this is a tactic used by the government to control them.

A few days later, the printer was raided again, this time by a different team of Home Ministry officers. These were very harsh actions meant to scare the printer and serve as a warning to me.

Several days after that, I received a call from one of the Home Ministry's officers summoning me to their office in Shah Alam for investigation. Ironically, the building I was summoned to was the same one where Teoh Beng Hock was found dead.

When I arrived, the officer led me to a room where I could see the confiscated copies of *Gedung Kartun*. He told me that I was being investigated under section 5(1) of the PPPA. If found guilty, I could be imprisoned for three years and fined RM20,000 (about US$5,000). I was interrogated for an hour. At the end, I told the officer: "You can ban my books, you can ban my cartoons, but you cannot ban my mind. I will keep drawing until the last drop of my ink."

This was to make it clear to him that there is no way he could stop me. I continued by saying: "Even if I don't have paper, I will use toilet tissue to draw. I will continue to draw because this is my right as a cartoonist."

This whole episode was not something I had planned. I actually wanted the magazine to be well distributed in the shops so that it could reach out to as many Malaysians as possible. The important thing was to get the message out to make people aware of what was going on in the country.

As a result of the raids, many bookshops were scared to sell the magazine. Some even began returning the copies to me. However, the reaction from the public was good, both locally and internationally, because this was a big issue. I received many emails from international cartoonists who said that my cartoons must have been very funny even though they had yet to read them.

In financial terms, sales of the magazine was poor as the bookshops were unable to sell them due to the Home Ministry's intimidation and harassment. I had to change my plan. So together with Jonos and a few cartoonists, we went to public places to sell the magazine directly to people. We went to mosques and shopping malls, and even to opposition political rallies. We also opened an online order site. People started to order the magazine by paying into my account and I posted the copies to them. We also started to use a subscription scheme, so people could subscribe to the magazine 12 months in advance; no one knew then that this would be the one and only issue.

However, the money from the sales was still not enough to cover the printing cost, let alone the entire operational cost. With limited monetary resources, it was difficult for me to use creative ways to deliver the message to the people. Nonetheless, it remains the duty of cartoonists to stand up against a corrupt regime and highlight the people's voice in their works.

The cover of *Gedung Kartun*.

I sketch with heart and draw with brain.

The raid on my office, the harassment against the printer and the intimidation of the bookstores were big challenges for me, but the fight through cartoons had to go on.

This was the earliest cartoon which got me in trouble during my school days at Sekolah Menengah Pendang, Kedah, for criticising my teachers in 1979.

This cartoon which criticised the country's defence system led the editor of *Berita Harian* to receive a show cause letter from the government in 1992.

Brainstorming session with the editorial team of *Gedung Kartun*.

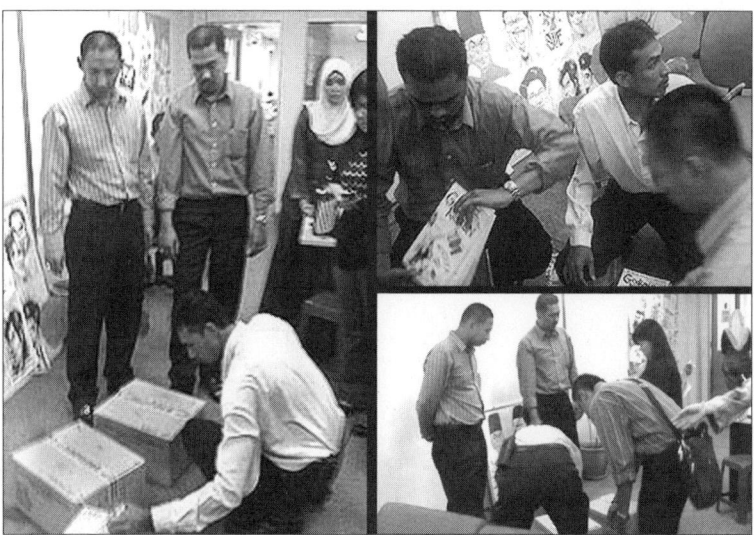

The raid by the Home Ministry officers at my office where they confiscated 408 copies of *Gedung Kartun*.

NEWS

Comic mag with Najib waving Mongolian flag seized

Salhan K Ahmad | Published: 25 Aug 2009, 12:53 pm | Modified: 25 Aug 2009, 12:53 pm

A⁺ A⁻

The Home Ministry today confiscated 408 copies of humour magazine Gedung Kartun which featured a caricature of Prime Minister Najib Abdul Razak waving a Mongolian flag and shouting Merdeka on the front cover of its inaugural issue.

The 10.45am raid was carried out by the ministry's Publication Control and Al Quran Text division at the publisher Sepakat Efektif Sdn Bhd in Brickfields, Kuala Lumpur.

According to ministry officials, the bi-weekly magazine, which

BERITA

Kilang cetak Gedung Kartun diserbu

Jimadie Shah Othman | Diterbitkan 26 Ogs 2009, 1:26 tengahari | Dikemaskini 26 Ogs 2009, 1:26 tengahari

A⁺ A⁻

kemaskini 4.09pm Selepas menyerbu pejabat *Gedung Kartun* semalam, Kementerian Dalam Negeri (KDN) hari ini menyerbu kilang percetakannya dan merampas plat reka bentuk cetakan majalah humor itu.

Selain merampas 408 naskhah majalah humor politik semalam, kementerian itu juga dikatakan turut mengadakan rampasan serupa di dua buah negeri.

Enam pegawai bahagian penerbitan KDN tiba di K Vin Publisher di Seri Kembangan, Serdang jam 11.30 pagi ini dan berada di situ selama hampir sejam.

News clippings from Malaysiakini. The second headline
in Malay reads "Gedung Kartun printer raided".

CHAPTER 3
PINCH OR PUNCH?

PINCH OR PUNCH?
Perak Darul Kartun

AFTER THE INVESTIGATION ON *GEDUNG KARTUN*, there was no further news whether they were going to charge me. Regardless of their decision, I decided to move on.

Personally, I contributed my cartoons to Malaysiakini twice a week. To maintain my staff, however, I needed to continue producing a magazine, but I was facing a big problem: my name and company had been blacklisted by the authorities after the *Gedung Kartun* episode.

To continue producing a cartoon magazine, I first needed a licence from the authorities and there was no way I could get it. How could I produce another cartoon magazine without facing any licence application issues?

After thinking about it and discussing with my team, particularly Jonos who had experience working in a publishing house, I came up with a solution. According to Malaysian law, a licence was needed if we produced a publication with the same title every month, but there was no need for a licence if we used a different title for each publication.

So the next publication was to have the same concept as *Gedung Kartun* and back-to-back satire. The only difference was the main theme. During that time, there was a political crisis in one of the states in Malaysia called Perak. I decided to name this publication *Perak Darul Kartun* (Perak the State of Cartoons), but the content still focused on main political issues in Malaysia, such as corruption, the murder of Altantuya, the conspiracy against Anwar Ibrahim, the Scorpene scandal and the wife of the prime minister, Rosmah Mansor.

However, by this time, several cartoonists who were involved with *Gedung Kartun* had already pulled out. They came to me and said that they were actually very supportive of my cause but they didn't want to create any trouble with the authorities. Some said they drew cartoons for *cari makan* (as a living). I responded by thanking them very much for their contributions. It was their choice whether they wanted to continue or not.

At the same time, I had received advice from senior Malaysian cartoonists who told me to slow down and soften my cartoons. They said my cartoons were too harsh towards the authorities. They also said my cartoons should not criticise Prime Minister Najib, but I could go after the other ministers. According to them, this was the reason I got into so much trouble with *Gedung Kartun*. They suggested that it would be better for me to criticise authorities in a subtle way and let the readers interpret the message behind it.

I told them thanks, but no thanks. My cartoons had to be very punchy. Why pinch when you can punch? We needed to punch because the situation was very bad in Malaysia. Pinching would never work because the government would not understand such an approach. They might understand punching, so we should punch hard. In fact, we should deliver a knockout. In order to do that, your punches have to be sharp. I said, I don't want to produce just another cartoon. I have always wanted to create cartoons that benefitted the people. And the cartoonists replied by saying good luck, but you might have to face the consequences. And I said, if this was the price I have to pay for making people laugh at a corrupt government, then so be it.

Our much smaller editorial team started work on the new publication. The content still focused on the main political issues in Malaysia — corruption, the killing of Altantuya, the conspiracy against Anwar and the scandal over the French submarines. As a bonus, I had political scientist and historian, Farish A. Noor, to contribute to the magazine. Farish, a renowned writer, did not contribute a written article but a cartoon of his own. This was something extraordinary and it was a great morale booster for me. Famous blogger, Hishammuddin Rais, also joined us.

Another stumbling block was to get a printer. K Vin Publisher, who had printed *Gedung Kartun*, didn't want to print anymore because of fear of the authorities after the raid on their premises. I had to search for another printer and, finally, Polar Vista Sdn Bhd agreed. On December 9, 2009, *Perak Darul Kartun* was released and it was launched a few days later, on December 13.

Nationwide distribution for *Perak Darul Kartun* began immediately. It became an instant hit and I think this was because of the *Gedung Kartun* controversy before it. I had to reprint it three times to fulfill popular demand. Legally, the authorities had no reason to stop me this time because *Perak Darul Kartun* was a book, and did not require a licence from the authorities.

Initially, everything went smoothly with no signs of any disruption from the authorities. There were no visits by Home Ministry officers and the printer was not raided. I was happy and thought to myself that this was the right way to overcome the law.

On June 24, 2010, I was shocked by the government's announcement to ban *Perak Darul Kartun*. They also banned another of my books, *1 Funny Malaysia*. The ban was under the Printing Presses and Publication Act (PPPA) and was officially recorded in the government's gazette. The reason given for the ban was because the content of the two books was detrimental to public order and could influence people to revolt against the government.

Following this, officers from the Home Ministry and the police started to conduct raids in bookstores nationwide. The bookstores were warned that they would be taken to court. Some of them received threats that their business licences would be affected if they continued to sell *Perak Darul Kartun*. I received several calls from bookstore owners in Penang, Johore, Perak and Selangor, complaining that their premises had been raided by the authorities and hundreds of copies of *Perak Darul Kartun* were seized. They said the Home Ministry officers and police threatened to bring them to court. They sought my advice on what they should do. I told them there was nothing I could do but please let me know if they were charged in court as I would try to help in any way I could.

More than a thousand copies of *Perak Darul Kartun* were confiscated nationwide. The distributor informed me that the bookstores had begun returning the books to them and they would send the copies back to my office. At that time, my studio looked like a warehouse with many bundles of books piled up.

In the *Gedung Kartun* episode, the authorities went after me on a licence issue. I thought that by avoiding this issue, I could continue. I was wrong. When *Perak Darul Kartun* was officially banned, it was confirmed that the issue was not about the licence. It was all about the government trying to stop me from producing funny and provocative cartoons.

First, they raided my office, and then they harassed my printers, banned my books and intimidated the bookstores. The more they wanted me to stop, the more motivated I became to continue. I would fight tooth and nail. More cartoons would come. I would also challenge the banning of *Perak Darul Kartun* in the court of law.

Let the battle begin.

One of the many cartoons in *Perak Darul Kartun*.

The cover of *Perak Darul Kartun*, published in December 2009.

With the cartoonists at the press conference to announce the publication of *Perak Darul Kartun*.

The launch of *Perak Darul Kartun* in Kuala Lumpur.

With fans at the launch of *Perak Darul Kartun*.

EVEN MY PEN HAS A STAND
1 Funny *Malaysia* and *Isu Dalam Kartun*

At this point in time, my motivations became bolder and more focused, but in order to fight effectively, my cartoons needed to have more engagement with the people. I wanted Malaysians to stand up with me against the corrupt. My objective was to get the people to understand how bad the corruption and misuse of power in Malaysia had become. I didn't want them to just let the issues happen without doing anything about it.

I realised that many people did not like politics, which was fine, but just because one didn't like politics doesn't mean that politicians should be allowed to do whatever they wanted to do. We can say that politics is dirty, but politics affects our lives. This mentality was not limited to people on the streets but the majority of Malaysians had the same attitude. What sickened me was that artists and cartoonists also had the same view and they didn't want to touch on political issues in their work. How could I make them understand that they too could play a part to push for a change?

I needed to come up with a slogan that could sum up the general lack of awareness about the governance of the country and the attitude of the people in one sentence. I need a punchy phrase to reflect this. I started to do a lot of deep thinking which took me several days of concentration. I focused on this a lot in my home, in my studio, in the bus and during meal times, but I could not find the right word.

One day, as I sat in my studio drawing, I suddenly got a clue. It was right in front of me on the drawing table. It was a mug holding a bunch of pens. I said to myself, this is what I am looking for.

The mug is where I put my pens before and after drawing. This mug functions as a pen stand. I came up with this philosophical phrase: "How can I be neutral? Even my pen has a stand".

This slogan reflected the importance for me as a human being and artist to take a clear stand. When we are faced with a moral crisis, there is no room to be neutral. Neutrality is escapism. For example, if you are at a bus stop and there is a lady beside you with a handbag, and a snatch thief suddenly appears and snatches her handbag in front of you, would you remain neutral?

By not doing anything, it means that you are indirectly allowing the snatcher to continue with his actions. The right thing to do would be to help the lady and apprehend the thief. By doing so, you are also taking a big risk if the snatcher has a weapon and you may get hurt, but you need to do this because it is your duty.

Apply this scenario to governing a country. If we remain neutral, we are giving the mandate to the corrupt authority to continue to be in power. That is why it is important to take a stand even though there are risks.

I took the risk to produce more stand-based cartoons. While I had a team that worked on the magazine, I continued my personal cartoon column with Malaysiakini. Around September 2009, I called up the editor of the news portal, Steven Gan, and his partner, Premesh Chandran, to see if they were interested to publish a book featuring cartoons from my column, which they agreed to. This was not the first time I had collaborated with them. Previously, we had co-produced a cartoon book called *Cartoons on Tun*.

In November 2009, I released *1 Funny Malaysia*. It was published by Malaysiakini through its subsidiary, Kinibooks, and printed by Vinlin Press Sdn Bhd. The cover of *1 Funny Malaysia* focused on the Scorpene submarine scandal, the shady dealings in the purchase of two submarines by the Malaysian government from a French company. Overall, the content of the book touched on political issues in Malaysia, such as corruption, misuse of power, political conspiracy against opposition leader Anwar Ibrahim, the lavish spending of the wife of the prime minister and the murder of the Mongolian model, Altantuya.

I had also added a disclaimer in the book that read: "All characters featured in this book are fictitious. They bear no resemblance to those involved in the Altantuya case or those who accepted bribes while negotiating submarine purchase deals. Neither do they bear resemblance to those who would pay millions to entice elected reps to jump ship. They certainly do not bear a resemblance to those whose wives consult with *bomohs* (shamans)."

Once again, the authorities conducted raids throughout bookstores nationwide. Starting in January 2010, they went from bookstore to bookstore, confiscating *1 Funny Malaysia* and warned booksellers that their licence could be revoked under the

Printing Presses and Publication Act (PPPA) if they continued selling my books.

I was told by vendors and bookstores that the raids were conducted by the police and the Home Ministry. During this time, there were also reports that some bookstores were threatened under a more serious law, the Sedition Act.

It should be noted that there is a huge difference between the PPPA and the Sedition Act.

Under the PPPA, the penalty was just a fine of a few hundred ringgit. Those who printed, published, sold, distributed, bought and owned my books could be penalized by a RM500 fine (around US$120). The Sedition Act, however, is criminal law. Those who print, publish, sell, distribute, buy and own my books could be jailed up to five years.

I think the authorities felt that the PPPA was not effective in stopping me. So they decided to upgrade their tactics by using a different law. The Sedition Act would scare more people away from supporting me.

I estimated that more than 1,000 books were taken away because the authorities went to many bookstores throughout Malaysia. There were also many unreported raids. Later, *1 Funny Malaysia* was also banned.

Meanwhile, I decided to produce another magazine, but I had to find a new way to get a licence from the government. My company, Sepakat Efektif Sdn Bhd, was already blacklisted by the government, so I could not apply for a licence through it.

The solution was to set up or find a different company with a different address and use it to apply for the licence. I realised my assistant, Jonos, had a sole proprietor company called Anillusca Ideas Enterprise. So I spoke to him and asked whether I could use his company which was registered under a different address. It was based in Gombak. Jonos said yes.

To get the licence, we needed to send a mock-up of the overall content of the magazine. I remembered that during the interrogation for *Gedung Kartun*, one of the issues raised by the officer then was about the mock-up for the magazine, which was different from the content that was published. I had sent a mock-up which showed non-political cartoons, while the actual publication of *Gedung Kartun* consisted of political cartoons.

This meant that to produce a political cartoon magazine, we needed to submit political cartoons in the mock-up. However, the submission procedure did not define or specify the messages that could be conveyed. So for *Isu Dalam Kartun*, I submitted political cartoons in the mock-up, but these depicted the government in a positive light.

After a few weeks, we received the licence and we began to produce *Isu Dalam Kartun*. *Isu Dalam Kartun* was a continuous teamwork project, following in the footsteps of *Gedung Kartun* and *Perak Darul Kartun*. The first volume was published in February 2010. In *Isu Dalam Kartun Volume 1*, we focused on Altantuya and how she was murdered, based on reports in the international media.

We illustrated the entire process of her murder. The magazine was released at the same time when the copies of *1 Funny Malaysia* and *Perak Darul Kartun* were being confiscated in bookstores nationwide. Not surprisingly, the authorities later confiscated *Isu Dalam Kartun Volume 1*.

In response, I released *Isu Dalam Kartun Volume 2* on March 24, 2010, and it was followed by *Isu Dalam Kartun Volume 3* on June 1 in the same year. More raids continued to happen. I felt they were not necessary because I had followed the direction set by the Home Ministry in submitting the mock-up for *Isu Dalam Kartun*, which had political cartoons.

The government cannot decide what kind of content we should draw and write. It is up to the cartoonists and the writers. So I wanted to find out if they were confiscating my cartoons because I had gone against any procedural rules or whether it was really because of the content of my cartoons.

A few weeks later, I found out. When questioned in Parliament by an Opposition lawmaker, the Home Ministry admitted that my magazines and books were taken away because of their content.

On June 24, 2010, the Home Ministry officially announced the banning of *Gedung Kartun*, *Perak Darul Kartun*, *1 Funny Malaysia*, *Isu Dalam Kartun Volume 1*, *Isu Dalam Kartun Volume 2* and *Isu Dalam Kartun Volume 3*.

In a press statement, Home Ministry secretary-general Mahmood Adam said my cartoons were banned because they were too dangerous for reading. According to him, the ban was gazetted on May 25, 2010.

I believe they wanted to see if I could be stopped from drawing. The official ban meant that according to law, no one could distribute, sell, buy or own my books. Vendors all over Malaysia began to return *Perak Darul Kartun* and *Isu Dalam Kartun* to me. Meanwhile, *1 Funny Malaysia* was returned to its publisher, Malaysiakini.

So during that time, my entire office was filled with all the returned copies. At the same time, many cartoonists left because they did not want to be part of this struggle anymore. I understood and thanked them for their contributions.

At this point, I started to have financial difficulties. Due to the ban, I was unable to sell the magazines. That led to an accumulation of debts with the printers. I owed the printers up to RM80,000 because the printing cost alone for one book could amount to RM20,000. I had published and printed more than 20,000 magazines and books and I couldn't sell them.

I had no choice but to let go of the cartoonists and the staff because I was unable to pay them. Only one person remained. She was my administrative staff. I had to close down my company, Sepakat Efektif Sdn Bhd.

Even without the support of the cartoonists and the staff, I wanted to continue to fight through cartoons and I knew I had to do it alone. I maintained a small office and continued to draw cartoons for Malaysiakini.

Now, I was faced with a new task — to challenge the banning of the six publications.

I started to have discussions with Malaysiakini together with our lawyers to initiate legal groundwork to challenge the ban. In my view, if the government was not happy with the publications, I would have been okay with it. If the Prime Minister felt that I had defamed him and his wife, he could have taken me to court and I would have been okay with that too. But to ban my books was unacceptable to me.

The ban on all of my books and magazines was unacceptable. A total ban meant that every page, including the front and back cover of the book, along with the copyright page, was detrimental to public order.

On July 26, 2010, Malaysiakini and I filed a legal suit to challenge the ban on *Perak Darul Kartun* and *1 Funny Malaysia* at the Kuala Lumpur High Court. I didn't file a legal suit for the three volumes of *Isu Dalam Kartun* because the owner of the company, Jonos, did not want to pursue the matter.

My philosophy on cartooning.

The battle in the courts would begin soon. I knew it would be very difficult for me to win in a Malaysian court because this was a politically motivated case, but it was important to continue because it would expose how fearful the government was of my cartoons and, at the same time, I hoped it would create an awareness in the public of how bad the situation had become in the country.

Isu Dalam Kartun Volume 2 was sold in bookstores before it was banned.

Isu Dalam Kartun was launched by the daughter of Anwar Ibrahim, Nurul Izzah (seated to my left).

The police confiscation list for *Gedung Kartun*, *Sumpah Dibumi Komisen (Isu Dalam Kartun Volume 1)*, *1 Funny Malaysia* and *Perak Darul Kartun*.

The book ban led me to sell my cartoon titles directly to people on the ground.

These six cartoon books were labelled as dangerous by the government.

A news clipping from the US media.

My cartoon on the government's fear of cartoonists.

CHAPTER 5
MY CARTOONS ARE DANGEROUS!

MY CARTOONS ARE DANGEROUS!
Battle at the courts

THE TRIAL FOR *PERAK DARUL Kartun* and *1 Funny Malaysia* began on April 27, 2011, at the Kuala Lumpur High Court. It went on for a few days, where arguments were exchanged from both sides.

During the trial, the government's lawyer, Noor Hisham Ismail, said both books had made very dangerous accusations against the government which could lead to riots on the streets. He said that the cartoons were also very disrespectful to the leaders of the country.

My lawyer, K Shanmuga, argued that the cartoons were uploaded on Malaysiakini eight months before the release of *1 Funny Malaysia*. From that time until the ban, there were no incidences of riots.

On July 14, 2011, the High Court Judge Rohaya Yusuf in her judgment rejected my challenge and said that the government was correct in banning my cartoons because they were sensitive in nature.

Malaysiakini and I did not agree and were not satisfied with Judge Rohaya's decision. So we decided to appeal to the Court of Appeal. The whole process from the day I filed the challenge at the High Court to the appeal at the Court of Appeal took more than three years.

On March 7, 2014, the Court of Appeal session began. It was before three judges, Datuk Mohamad Ariff Md Yusof, Datuk Varghese George Varughese and Datuk Tengku Maimun Tuan Mat. During the trial, the judges and lawyers from both sides went through both books and argued about my cartoons page by page.

When one of the judges asked the government's lawyers to show examples of what they meant by bad cartoons in *Perak Darul Kartun* and *1 Funny Malaysia*, the lawyers showed some of my cartoons which mocked the judiciary. They tried their best to convince the judges about how bad my cartoons were.

At one point in the proceedings, Justice Mohamad Ariff had interjected by saying that my cartoons were works of satire, hence it was okay to make fun of the judiciary or politicians.

On October 9, 2014, the Court of Appeal in a landmark judgment instructed the government to lift the ban on *Perak Darul Kartun* and *1 Funny Malaysia*. The three judges said that the government's interpretation of my cartoons could not be turned to law.

In his judgment, Justice Mohamad Ariff said:

> Admittedly, the respondent (home minister) had submitted that the cartoons are rude, I would describe it as crude. If it is contemptuous, they are open to sue the appellant. This is a better alternative than an outright

ban. These are political cartoons, but can cartoons, per se, disrupt public order? Cartoons exaggerate, satirise, and parody life, including political life. When read (more likely, glanced through), they would tickle the ribs, perhaps evoke a chuckle and make one reflect for a momentary instance the humorous side. Quite often, the reader is drawn to it by its incisive wit.

Justice Varghese, in his supporting judgment, said:

> Works termed generally as 'graffiti' have evolved to be tolerated and acclaimed art form. Such passive material was, in any case, open to varying interpretations or levels of appreciation by a beholder or reader. To say that such material was incendiary and had stirred up strife and disturbed public order was, in my view, not a supportive conclusion in the circumstances, by any reasonable criteria. However, it cannot be denied that, insofar as the courts are concerned, they (the government) are armed with sufficient powers to protect or safeguard their integrity against any contempt, either on its own motion or at the instance of the honourable Attorney-General or any aggrieved party. There are in existence a legal process and powers to effectively deal with any affront to the court's dignity or any attempt at interference with the administration of justice.

The judges also criticised the government for banning my books. Justice Varghese said:

> The minister has here acted unreasonably and irrationally in issuing the orders as he did. With due respect, the learned judge sitting in the review court below (the High

Court) could have granted the order of certiorari applied and quashed the minister's order.

What the judges meant was that the government's opinion that my cartoons were dangerous were only a matter of their own interpretation.

I welcomed the decision. It was a landmark decision by the Court of Appeal and set a precedence for future cases concerning book bans, especially with regards to works of satire. I was so happy because, finally, the fight in the courtroom had paid off. I thought it was all over.

The government, however, still wanted to continue the fight against me. They submitted an appeal to the highest court in Malaysia, the Federal Court, to review the Court of Appeal's decision.

Perak Darul Kartun and *1 Funny Malaysia* became the first cartoon books in the history of Malaysia to be tried at the Federal Court.

On November 11, 2015, the Federal Court made a judgment to maintain the Court of Appeal's decision. The five-member panel led by Justice Md Raus Sharif instructed the government to lift the ban on my books and return them to me.

It was a hard-fought victory for me. By then, the case had gained international attention all over the world.

Discussing legal strategies with my lawyers.

At the Kuala Lumpur High Court during the filing of my book ban challenge in July 2010.

News clipping from Malaysian media, *The Star*.

Speaking to reporters at the Kuala Lumpur High Court during the trial of my banned books.

I drew the Court of Appeal judges during the *1 Funny Malaysia* book ban challenge.

A news clipping from a Malaysian daily, *The Sun* — October 9, 2014.

CHAPTER 6
CARTOON-O-PHOBIA

CARTOON-O-PHOBIA
Sedition and handcuffs

THE RAIDS ON MY OFFICE, printers and bookstores, together with the confiscation and banning of my books, had a very humourous side to them. So I thought of producing a book covering the whole episode.

The title had to be one word to describe a government that is afraid of cartoons. In the West, you have Islamophobia.

On September 21, 2010, I released *Cartoon-O-Phobia*, a book that poked fun at the government for their comical behaviour towards me and my cartoons.

The launch was planned for September 24, 2010, at 8pm at the Selangor Chinese Assembly Hall in Kuala Lumpur. The announcement of the launch was made through social media and news portals.

For the launch, I didn't want to do anything normal, like breaking glass or ribbon cutting. I decided to draw one big cartoon on the prime minister and his wife, Rosmah. I depicted her with big hair. The idea was for the book to be pulled out from the hair.

So I had to do a collage drawing for this purpose, and this meant the drawing had to have two layers. In order to do that, a few friends and I went to collect real human hair from barber shops around the city. The hair was glued on top of Rosmah's head.

For me, I felt this would make an interesting gimmick for the launch. All went smoothly. The final artwork was sent to the printers for printing and I was excited to see the results.

On the launch day, I received 66 copies of *Cartoon-O-Phobia* from Malaysiakini. I placed them near the front door of my office. At around 4pm, I was in my room preparing my speech for the launch when suddenly, I saw eight policemen storming into my office.

When they came in, two stationed themselves at the back door of my office, thinking that I would run away. The leader then came to me and introduced himself as ASP Arikrishnan Apparau from Brickfields Police Station.

He said he had received a report that I was publishing a seditious book, and he wanted to confiscate all 66 copies of *Cartoon-O-Phobia* in my office. I told Arikrishnan not to touch anything because I wanted to get my lawyer.

I called my lawyer, Latheefa Koya, and I was very fortunate that she was near my office. She said she would arrive in 10 minutes.

At this point, the police began to confiscate my books. They also went to search another room and found the collage artwork of

Najib and Rosmah. They seized it. I argued with Arikrishnan that if he was here for my books, why was he confiscating the collage?

He replied that he had the right to do that under the Sedition Act, and that was when I knew that the raid was conducted under that criminal law. I was so scared because this meant jail for me. Even though my office had been raided before, it had been under the PPPA, which is civil law for which the punishment is not a jail term. Then I called my wife to prepare my daily medication.

When Latheefa arrived, she asked Arikrishnan about the offence I had committed. He replied that I had produced a seditious cartoon book, which was an offence under the Sedition Act. For that, he was going to arrest me and bring me to the police station.

Finally, knowing for sure that I would be taken to the police station, I told the police to give me a few minutes because I needed to use the laptop to inform my family and friends. Instead, I took this chance to publish the news that I was being arrested through my Facebook and Twitter accounts.

The news began circulating.

After that I was handcuffed. Arikrishnan also instructed his men to confiscate all 66 copies of *Cartoon-O-Phobia* and the artwork. I was brought downstairs where two police cars were waiting. I could see everybody in my neighbourhood coming out to see what was happening. I was pushed into one of the cars and brought to Brickfields Police Station, which was located 10 minutes from my office.

When I arrived, I was brought into a room where I waited for half an hour and after that, Arikrishnan came and told me that they were going to send me to another police station.

After that I was taken to a total of seven police stations: Brickfields, Petaling Jaya, Petaling Jaya Utara, Bukit Puchong, Serdang, Sepang, Seri Kembangan and, finally, to the Kuala Lumpur International Airport (KLIA) police lock-up. I didn't know the motive for shifting me around to different police stations, but I suspected that it was done to confuse my fans.

I was arrested at 6pm. The launch which was scheduled for 8pm went ahead. So I think the police were worried that if I was arrested and detained at Brickfields Police Station, which is close to the launch venue, my fans would go to the station to protest the arrest. It was only a 20-minute drive away, while the KLIA police lock-up was more than an hour away.

Finally, at around midnight, I arrived at the KLIA lock-up. My lawyer Latheefa arrived soon after. The police called both of us into a room and the officer asked me, "How many books did you actually print?" At this point, Latheefa said to me that I had the right not to answer the question. It looked like they were trying to get rid of all the *Cartoon-O-Phobia* books. After that, I was handcuffed and sent to the police lock-up downstairs. I was detained in the same room as drug addicts, drug pushers and all kinds of serious criminals. I was given only a pair of shorts and a t-shirt. Nothing else.

The situation in the lock-up was very bad. I had to sleep on the cold, hard cement floor. The toilets were open without door and walls, and all the inmates could see what you were doing in the toilet.

I couldn't sleep that night. As the lock-up was close to the airport, I could hear the noisy sound of planes taking off and landing. I didn't know what to do in the lock-up.

Then, I saw one of the inmates writing something on a piece of paper using the inner nib of a pen. I borrowed it from him and started to sketch the situation in the lock-up. I had to sit in a corner to avoid being noticed by the police.

While I was under arrest that night, the launch of the book went on as planned. As the news of my arrest had spread widely, many fans attended the launch event. The situation was very tense due to the heavy police presence. There were no books at the venue because the publisher was too scared to bring them.

There were many people who wanted to buy *Cartoon-O-Phobia*. So one of my assistants took down their contact details and promised to deliver the books by post. The editor of Malaysiakini, Steven Gan, and Opposition politician, Nizar Jamaluddin, updated the crowd on my latest situation. My wife, Fazlina Rosley, spoke on my behalf. This must have been the funniest and strangest book launch in history — being the first time a book was launched without any books or the author!

Earlier in the evening, after my arrest, a separate team of policemen had also raided the printer. The purpose was to confiscate the rest of the books.

By then, the printer had read the news and hid the books. When the police arrived, they told the police that they didn't know where the books were as the stock had been delivered to the publisher and author.

However, the police found the printing invoice and discovered that 3,000 copies of *Cartoon-O-Phobia* had been printed.

The next morning, the police brought me to the Magistrate's Court in Sepang to obtain a remand order to extend my detention.

The police had informed my lawyer about the location of the court only that morning; she had to drive more than an hour from Kuala Lumpur to find the place. This was in 2010, when there were no applications such as Google Maps or Waze to help you find the location of places. One can only imagine how difficult it must have been for her to find the court.

It was a Saturday, so the court was only open for half a day until 12pm. In the court with me were a few other detainees who were waiting for their remand orders. The judge handled their cases one by one, whilst waiting for my lawyer to arrive.

When all the other cases were done at 11.30am, it was my turn. The judge asked me where my lawyer was. I said I didn't know because my phone was not with me. He said the courtroom was about to close and I had half an hour to get my lawyer there. After waiting for a few more minutes, she still did not arrive. As time was running out, I requested the judge to allow me to represent myself. He asked me if I was sure about this. I said, yes. It was not difficult because I had been to the courts many times and this was just about my remand order.

I said to myself, since the law in Malaysia is so cartoonish, there's nothing wrong with a cartoonist becoming a lawyer.

The police started the case by saying that they needed to detain me for a few days in the lock-up for investigations. They said I had produced a book which was seditious in nature. Section 3(3) of the Sedition Act stated that I could be jailed for three years and fined RM20,000 (about US$5,000) if found guilty.

It was then my turn to speak. I asked the judge how the police knew if my cartoons were seditious or not. *Cartoon-O-Phobia* was not even launched or sold when I was arrested. Unless the police had read the book first before arresting me, it would not have made any sense. The court had no choice but to release me on bail.

I was brought back to the police station, made to sit on the floor at the corner of the office and handcuffed for eight hours. The police asked me where the rest of the books were, to which I replied that I didn't know because I had only received 66 copies, all of which they had already taken.

Then the officer informed me that they would bring me to the Malaysiakini office to get the rest of the books. At this point, my other lawyer, Fadiah, arrived to see me. I whispered to her that the police would be going to Malaysiakini soon, and told her to inform them.

In the afternoon, my wife and another lawyer, Murni, paid me a visit. They brought lunch for me. During that time, I told Murni to secretly take a photo of me in handcuffs and upload it onto social media.

At around 3pm, the police went to Malaysiakini's office to look for the books. They didn't bring me as planned. I believe Fadiah's message was received by the Malaysiakini team as they had hidden the books somewhere else.

After an hour of interrogation, the police left Malaysiakini's office empty-handed. The police had to make do with 66 copies. I was finally released at 6pm on September 25, 2010.

In this incident, the government changed their tactic. During the first raid at my office, the Home Ministry officers came and the law used was the Printing Presses and Publication Act (PPPA). For the second raid, it was the police who came and the law used was the Sedition Act with detention and arrest.

The scare tactics against the printer were also intensified. During the *Gedung Kartun* raid, they had gone after the manager of the printing company. This time, they went after the owner of the licence. The owner received a very strong warning that his business licence would be revoked if he continued to print my books in the future and he could be charged under the Sedition Act.

Several months after that, I received the Courage in Editorial Cartooning award by Cartoonists Rights Network International (CRNI). The award was presented to me in Florida on July 12, 2011. CRNI is the only body that monitors issues faced by persecuted cartoonists around the world. They take care of more than 600 cartoonists. CRNI was initiated by its director, Dr Robert Russell. According to Dr Russell, my cartoons were a weapon to fight corruption and abuse of power in the government.

After that, I published another book, *1 Moolaysia*, which was released on March 22, 2012.

On June 15, 2011, I filed a suit at the High Court in Kuala Lumpur to challenge my unlawful arrest and the confiscation of my books and the collage artwork during the raid on *Cartoon-O-Phobia*. The trial began on January 18, 2012.

During the proceedings, Arikrishnan was the first witness for the government. He said that every page of *Cartoon-O-Phobia* was seditious and could create hatred, misunderstanding and confusion about the Malaysian government amongst the public.

My lawyer, N Surendran, questioned if that was so, why did the police have to confiscate the collage as well? It was not part of the book. The trial went on for more than one and a half years.

On judgment day, on July 31, 2012, Justice Vazeer Alam Mydin Meera ruled that the police was correct in arresting me but wrong to confiscate my books and the collage. The judge instructed the police to return my books and the artwork to me.

Both the government and I appealed against the decision to the Court of Appeal. I appealed because I felt my arrest was illegal. The government appealed because they did not want to return my books and artwork. My lawyer said this was known as a cross-appeal and it was very rare. I said this was cartoon-o-phobia.

The case was now in the hands of the Court of Appeal and the judgment date was set on November 1, 2013. When delivering the decision, Justices Abdul Aziz Abdul Rahim, Mohd Ariff Md Yusof and David Wong maintained that my arrest was lawful.

The judges also instructed the police to return my books and the collage on the same condition as before. The next process for me was to go back to the High Court to obtain the letter of returning order.

On March 23, 2015, I was accompanied by another lawyer, Michelle Yesudas, to Salak Tinggi Police Station in Selangor to take back my books and the collage artwork. At the police station, the police returned all 66 copies of *Cartoon-O-Phobia*. After checking them one by one, they were found to be in good condition and I signed the *surat serahan* (delivery form). For the collage artwork, however,

I signed off on the form with a note: "Received with damage". What type of damage was sustained? This artwork was a mix of drawing with real human hair pasted on it. During the trial, the police had to produce the artwork as evidence which they would fold and unfold. Each time they opened it in the courtroom, the hair would fall out.

I took the police to court. This time for damaging my collage artwork. The government had to be responsible for the damage. If they had wanted to confiscate my artwork, it should at least have been treated with respect. I felt that it was unnecessary to have confiscated my collage, but if they had to take it, then they should have taken proper care of it.

After the filing of the suit, my lawyers and the government lawyers began to discuss how to estimate the quantum of the damage. Jokingly, I said it could be calculated by counting how many strands of hair had fallen off the artwork. If one strand of hair cost RM100, 1,000 strands would be RM100,000! Seriously, though, as the value of the artwork was very subjective, it was very difficult to calculate the damage.

The only person who could determine the value was the expert in this field. So I contacted a friend, Dr Hew Kuan Yau, from Penang's Asia Comic Cultural Museum. He is the only person in Malaysia who is qualified to make an assessment. He agreed to testify as my witness in court. He produced a letter of assessment stating that my artwork was worth at least RM20,000 (US$5,000).

During the second round of exchanging documents for the case, the lawyer for the police realised that we had a letter of assessment from an expert, so they said they needed more time to get an expert to help them. I believe they wrote to the National Art Gallery, but the people there are not experts in cartoons because everything that is exhibited in the gallery are fine art pieces, not cartoons.

I believe this was the reason they didn't want to argue about this in the next session in court. They offered to pay me RM8,000 for the damage done. I said no and told them the matter would be brought to court. Feeling apprehensive that prolonging the case would only hurt them in the long run, they finally offered me RM18,000, which I felt was still a very low figure for the collage. However, after discussing with my lawyers, we agreed to the amount. The important thing is that in agreeing to pay me that amount, it shows that the police have admitted their mistake. On April 11, 2017, the High Court ordered the government and the police to pay me RM18,000 (US$4,500) in damages. It was another victory for me.

As the latest raid on my office and the printer were the most serious to date, this news was circulated among the printers' network. As a result, printers no longer dared to print my books because they were afraid of losing their licences.

After that, when I wanted to publish another book, *Even My Pen has a Stand*, I was unable to find a printer who dared to print it. According to the law, the printer's name has to be printed on the third page of the book, and if I did that, the police would immediately pay the printer a visit. So for the new book, I had to search around Malaysia for printers. I asked printers in Kuala Lumpur who declined, I went to printers in Seremban and Penang, but they also declined. I had to spend three months just searching for a printer.

Finally, I managed to find a small printer in Pudu who was willing to print the new cartoon book. He only agreed to one single print run, after which he didn't want to print any more.

Even My Pen has a Stand was launched on July 2, 2011.

One of my artworks in *Cartoon-O-Phobia*.

The cover of *Cartoon-O-Phobia*.

The banner for the launch of *Cartoon-O-Phobia*.

The police raid and confiscation of my books and artwork from my office in Kuala Lumpur.

I was arrested and taken to Brickfields Police Station.

I was brought to seven different police stations in a police van.

I was finally detained at the KLIA police lock-up.

This picture was taken by my lawyer during the interrogation session at the police station.

I secretly drew this during my detention to show the conditions in my cell.

My wife Fazlina has been very helpful when I faced hard times. Here, she brought me fried rice for my lunch during my detention at the police lock-up.

At the court with my lawyers during the filing of my challenge against the government.

Together with my lawyers at the trial of my unlawful arrest at the Kuala Lumpur High Court.

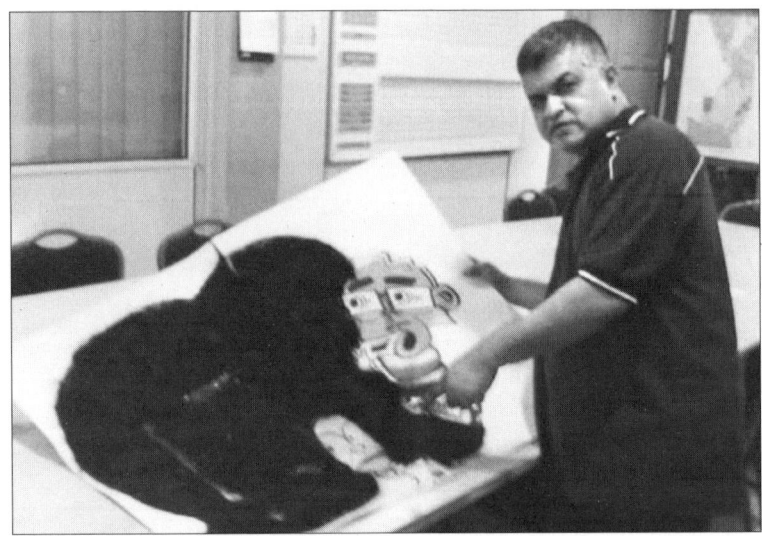

My confiscated artwork of Najib and Rosmah was badly damaged by the police.

I received the Courage in Editorial Cartooning Award from CRNI in Florida on July 12, 2011.

The cover of my then latest book, *Even My Pen has a Stand*.

Despite fear of the police, the public still attended the launch for *Even My Pen has a Stand*.

CHAPTER 7
ARREST OF THE ASSISTANTS

ARREST OF THE ASSISTANTS
Pirates of the Carry-BN and The Conspiracy to Imprison Anwar

I WAS RELIEVED THAT THERE were still printers willing to print my books. This enabled me to produce two more titles. The first one, *Lawak & Lawan*, was launched on December 14, 2012, and was followed by *Ini-Kartun-Lah* on April 28, 2013.

The title *Lawak & Lawan* means "joking and fighting". This book was released prior to the 13th general elections. The focus was on corruption. There was a note on the cover giving a strong message to the people to kick the ruling regime out. The note read, "Edisi gelak guling-guling. Sambil gelak, sambil guling kerajaan." (Rolling on the floor laughing edition. While laughing, push for a change.) The launch was officiated by Lembah Pantai member of parliament, Nurul Izzah, who is also the daughter of Anwar Ibrahim. She has been very supportive of me and my books, and continues to do so to this day.

Ini-Kartun-Lah was published during the election campaign. The title was taken from the popular slogan among opposition supporters, "Ini Kalilah" (This is the time). However, the ruling coalition, Barisan Nasional, won the elections.

Months after that, on November 17, 2013, I released a cartoon book, *Pirates of the Carry-BN*. I portrayed the country's leaders as pirates on the cover and named it to parody the famous film, *Pirates of the Caribbean*.

Pirates of the Carry-BN was received by the Library of Congress in Washington DC, in the US. They held a gathering for me and I handed the book over to the library. This library is one of the biggest research libraries in the world.

A year later, I released another cartoon book, *The Conspiracy to Imprison Anwar* on May 23, 2014. I also released a Bahasa Malaysia version and named it *Komplot Penjarakan Anwar*. The book was about the plan by Mahathir and Najib to put Anwar in jail from 1998 to 2014.

During this time, international attention on me increased, especially in the United States, and I was invited to speak at several universities and organisations around the country.

It was at this point that the Malaysian government started to use different tactics against me. First, they banned *Pirates of the Carry-BN* and *The Conspiracy to Imprison Anwar* without my knowledge. I only found out after my arrest in 2016. Second, they began going after people closer to me.

On November 6, 2014, during Anwar's trial at the Palace of Justice, three of my assistants were arrested for selling *Pirates of the Carry-BN* and *The Conspiracy to Imprison Anwar*. Norliza Mohd Kassim, Ridzaldy Rafie and Raja Norita were taken to Putrajaya Police Station and investigated under the Printing Presses and Publications Act, the Sedition Act and the Penal Code.

The arrest happened earlier in the evening. There was a huge crowd during the trial. The police waited for everyone to leave around 6pm before they arrested my three assistants and put them in a police van.

Somehow, one supporter realised they had been arrested. The van had not yet left because the police officers were busy confiscating the books. The man approached Norita, who was seated nearest to a window in the van and asked Norita for my phone number to inform me. I was at home at that time. He then rang me twice, but I missed his calls.

Realising that I did not pick up my phone, Norita gave him another number which belonged to my wife. This was when the police got into the van and began driving off. The man asked Norita whose number it was and she shouted loudly, "Zunar's wife!"

I was puzzled that there were various news articles circulating that my wife had been arrested. My wife was in Port Dickson during that time attending a course, and she began receiving many texts from her family and friends. She was also surprised and didn't know what was happening.

I called the editor of one of the newspapers, *Sinar Harian*, which had run a story on the arrest. I told her that her reporter had misreported on the matter and explained that the woman in the police van was my assistant and not my wife. She said she had picked up the story from the news agency, *Bernama*.

So I called *Bernama*, asking them how they could have made such a report without first checking with me. The editor said the information was given by the police. I said that *Bernama* had to make a correction. Later, a reporter from *Bernama* called me to get my clarifications on the matter. I told the news agency to issue an apology and to make it clear that my wife had not been arrested. *Bernama* then issued a statement of apology. Malaysiakini reported, "*Bernama* minta maaf kepada Zunar". (*Bernama* apologises to Zunar.)

I tried to figure out how the police could have mistaken Norita for my wife. I found out later it was because when Norita was in the police van and had shouted out "Zunar's wife", what she had meant was that it was Zunar's wife's phone number that she had given, but the police thought Norita was saying that she was my wife.

Norliza, Ridzaldy and Norita were taken to Putrajaya Police Station and questioned for several hours. After 1am, they were released.

This was another tactic to stop me. Before this, they had tried to go after the printers, the bookstores, they had banned my books and put me in the lock-up, and had tried all kinds of harassment.

Admittedly, this was a very hard time for me. When they banned my books and went after the bookstores and printers, they managed to stop the open sale of my books. This made my situation very difficult financially. This could not go on. I had to find a way to sell my books, one way or another, but I didn't know how.

At this point, surprisingly and unexpectedly, I was approached by one of my fans, Mubashar Aftab. He called himself Shah. He offered to set up a website on a volunteer basis to help me sell my books online. Shah actually had a small, full-time digital business and he did this for me because he sincerely wanted to help me. So he and another fan, Aron, set up a website called Zunar.my for the online sale and ordering of my books. It was also a platform where I could upload new cartoons and update my fans on the latest news. The business transaction part of the website was registered under online gateway, MOLPay. It went very well and the orders started to come in.

However, the government wanted to stop me from selling my books online, too. Their purpose was to ensure that my books wouldn't exist and wouldn't be distributed. In early November that year, Shah and Aron informed me that they had received a call from the police asking who was managing my website. I told Shah to cooperate with the police because this website was set up according to the law and we were doing business legally. After that, Shah informed me that he had received another call from the police asking him to report to Dang Wangi Police Station on November 13, the same year, to be investigated under the Sedition Act.

Following that, Shah came to see me privately and said he wanted to quit as my web master. He was afraid now that the police were after him, his other business would be affected. According to him, the decision was a difficult one, but he made it after a long discussion with his family.

Originally, Shah had offered to build the website from scratch and run it for me on a volunteer basis without any payment in return. He received a small commission from the sales of the books, but he did not make much money helping me.

I said to him that if he wanted to quit, I could not stop him, it was his decision. I also could not do anything to protect him, but I explained to him that the reason the police had called him up was because they wanted to get to me: I was the government's real target. I told him that even if they brought him to court, he would only serve as a witness to strengthen their case against me. This was their tactic to stop me. The next morning, Shah told me that he would continue to run my website.

On November 13, he reported to Dang Wangi Police Station. I called up a lawyer to accompany and help him during the investigation. I told Shah to follow the lawyer's advice during the interrogation. Among the questions the police asked him was who handled the website, who did the uploading of the materials, who had the password and access to my website and what was the structure of the website, what was MOLPay and what was Shah's relationship to me. They also asked if he was paid to do this. For these questions, he was advised by the lawyer not to answer them but only to answer in court.

A week after that, on November 20, 2014, Shah informed me that he had received an email from MOLPay informing him that the police had raided their office in Petaling Jaya.

In the email, the company told Shah that the police had demanded the names of customers who had purchased my books via the website. The police had threatened to charge the company under the Sedition Act for helping me to sell my books. MOLPay also informed that they had no choice but to reveal the information to the police.

I told Shah to reply to MOLPay that in giving the names to the police, they had breached the contract we had signed with them. The contract stated clearly that the privacy of my customers was protected under the Personal Data Protection Act. I asked Shah to inform them that I might take legal action against them if there was no solution to this.

During this time, there was tension between myself and the company.

A few months after that, the police called me for investigation at Dang Wangi Police Station. They investigated me under section 4 of the Sedition Act for publishing *Pirates of the Carry-BN* and *The Conspiracy to Imprison Anwar*. After the interrogation, the person in charge, ASP Suta, told me that she was investigating another case related to me, but she didn't want to tell me which case she was referring to.

The next morning, when I was in my studio, my phone rang. The name appearing on the phone was ASP Sutha. When I answered the call, she asked, "Is it MOLPay?" I replied, "No, this is Zunar." She immediately hung up.

I knew then she had wanted to call MOLPay but had mistakenly called me instead. I realised this was the case Suta had referred to the day before. That was when I knew they would continue to investigate MOLPay.

I immediately called Shah and asked him to send a letter to warn the company that if they did not protect my customers, I would sue them. I felt that MOLPay had to play a responsible role in protecting my customers. MOLPay eventually informed me that they did not disclose the names of my customers.

A couple of months after that, on January 28, 2015, when I was on a speaking tour in London, the police raided my office in Pudu. They confiscated a total of 155 copies of *Pirates of the Carry-BN*, *The Conspiracy to Imprison Anwar* and *Komplot Penjarakan Anwar*. The police said my books were seized under Section 2 of the Printing Presses and Publications Act, Section 4(1)(c) of the Sedition Act and Section 500 of the Penal Code.

Usually when the police seized my books, I would have to sign a confiscation form, but because I was away, the police asked a managing director from a neighbouring office to sign the form.

I had to shift office several times. Despite the difficulties, my assistants Jonos and Azman MatNoh could still afford to smile while helping me.

The managing director suggested to me that I move out because this was very difficult for his company's business. They were afraid that if each time the police came when I was not around, they would have to sign the form for me. They did this once and they didn't want to do it again.

So I had to move my office to another location. This was my second office after the one in Brickfields.

Despite the threat and pressure from the police and the government,
I still managed to come out with these three books:
Lawak & Lawan, Ini-Kartun-Lah and *Pirates of the Carry-BN*.

Presenting *Pirates of the Carry-BN* to a representative of the Library of Congress in Washington DC.

At the launch of *Pirates of the Carry-BN*, I dressed up as a pirate.

I mocked the judge during Anwar Ibrahim's trial.

The cover of *The Conspiracy to Imprison Anwar*.

The police arrested my assistant, Ridzaldy Rafie (middle), who was selling my books on a motorcycle.

One of my assistants, Norliza Mohd Kassim @ Yong was also arrested.

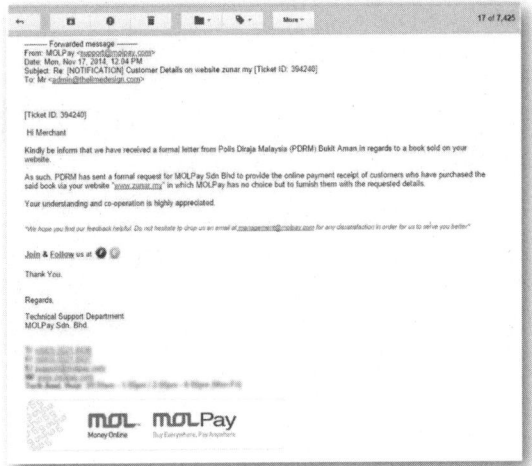

The email from MOLPay showed the police demanding a list of people who purchased my books online.

My webmaster, Mubashar Aftab, was also investigated by the police.

At the entrance of Dang Wangi Police Station during the investigations on my cartoon books.

Pirates of the Carry-BN (left) and *The Conspiracy to Imprison Anwar* were the latest books to be banned.

TALENT IS NOT A GIFT
Of Birkin, rings and diamonds

AT THIS JUNCTURE, I HAD already produced thousands of cartoons and 13 books, but I felt that they didn't create enough impact for the people on the ground. I began thinking that I had to develop a new way to draw cartoons. All this while, my cartoons had focused too much on politics and the message did not travel widely to the people. They did not contribute much in terms of change in Malaysia. As a result, Najib and Barisan Nasional won the 13th general elections on May 5, 2013, and they managed to stay in power.

The approach to cartooning needed to be reconstructed. I wanted my cartoons to reach more people. How would I do this?

I realised that in most of my cartoons, the angle was mainly political. The issues highlighted were from the perspective of politicians and they were presented at their level of communication. Issues such as policies and what they said in Parliament were turned into cartoons, but the people couldn't relate to such things.

When I meet Malaysians, they tend to say that politicians are all the same. Politics and politicians have nothing to do with their lives despite my explanation that awareness of politics is important. This was their mindset and I felt that I was unable to change it overnight, but this was the key to my breakthrough.

After thinking about it for a long time, I came up with the concept of cartoons for the people. This meant that in terms of visuals and angles, I had to focus more on issues from the people's perspective.

Visually, I began to put in more of people's characters into my cartoons. For instance, when I draw on corruption issues, I would show politicians taking money from the people's pockets. I wanted them to understand that corruption was not a political issue but that we were actually the ones who were paying for their corruption. From then on, it was cartoons for the people. No more typical political cartoons. This concept was the result of long and deep thinking about my own philosophy on cartooning.

People go to university to get certificates to become lawyers, doctors, engineers, and many other professionals. But to become a cartoonist, I didn't need to go to university. Why? Because I was born with this talent.

My talent is godsent. Artists use their talents for many purposes. Some use it to make money, some to become famous, others to become a pioneer or creator of something new. But for me, talent is not a gift, it is a responsibility. This means that I'm not supposed to use this talent for my own monetary gain, but for the benefit of the people.

So I began to remove the copyright notice from my cartoons. My decision is one that other artists might not agree with, but I felt that the people should be free to share and use my cartoons in any means possible to get the message out. These cartoons were for the people and I wanted them to have access to them. More access means more impact.

The visual aspect of the cartoons also changed. I tried to find an object that the people could relate to. I also wanted to find a symbol that represented the issue of corruption. How would I make my cartoons simple and yet be able to send the message into the hearts of the people?

I found that symbol in Rosmah, Najib's wife.

She was very powerful and led an extravagant lifestyle. I noticed that people were more entertained with my cartoons when I drew her than when I drew Najib. Not only is she funny, she is also very "cartoonable". This was why I began introducing Rosmah into my cartoons.

I used her diamond ring to represent lavish spending and wastage of public funds. This was the usage of visual language to make people understand and realise what was happening, and it's one of the ways that artists use symbols in their artwork. She said she had saved her money from a young age to buy it. For me, it didn't matter. I began to draw her with the ring. From then on, whenever she appeared in my cartoons, she would have this ring on. In some cartoons, she is not even in the frame, but her ring is in the picture.

In later cartoons, I began introducing Rosmah's Birkin handbags and a price tag on her hair. She had famously said that it had cost her

RM1,200 (US$300) to do her hair, but this amount also represented the minimum salary many Malaysians were demanding.

When people saw my cartoons of Rosmah, they understood the issues taking place in Malaysia.

By drawing for the people and using Rosmah as the subject, I received more responses and feedback from the people.

Many Malaysians did not really know the details of the corruption issues such as the 1Malaysia Development Berhad (1MDB) scandal. They didn't know or understand what or where the British Virgin Islands were. They didn't know about Petro Saudi and didn't understand the term "offshore investment". But they could easily understand the ring, her handbags and her hair with the price tag which represented corruption, abuse of power and misuse of political funds. When Malaysians saw the ring, they understood the message in my cartoons.

Based on these new concepts, I came up with a new cartoon book called *Ros in Kangkong Land*, which was published in early 2015. In the book, I said I was lucky because in Malaysia, we had Rosmah. She had given me so much inspiration for my cartoons.

She's godsent to me, she's cartoonable and what I needed to do was get my pen and pencil ready, watch television and wait for her to say something. Then I could start to draw. Sometimes, though, she disappeared for one or two months from public view and the news. I would then have to pray to God, "Please make her say something. I am out of ideas now."

As there was a huge response from the public for her cartoons, the authorities came down harder on me.

Unlike the previous books which I was able to launch before the authorities either banned them or arrested me, for this book, their actions were so aggressive I couldn't even launch it. Twice I had tried to hold an event to launch it, but on both occasions, February 14 and 28, 2015, the police came and cordoned off the area to stop the launch. They had threatened to arrest me on both occasions and I had to cancel the event.

In my later cartoons, I didn't use the word "Ros". Instead, she was known as "Mah", because this was a new word which had not yet been used to refer to her. So "Mah" is synonymous with my cartoons and became my trademark.

The following are some of the "Cartoon for the People" images that introduced Rosmah as an object to help people understand more about corruption in Malaysia.

The cover of *Ros in Kangkong Land*.

Even the barcode for the book was designed based on Rosmah's hair.

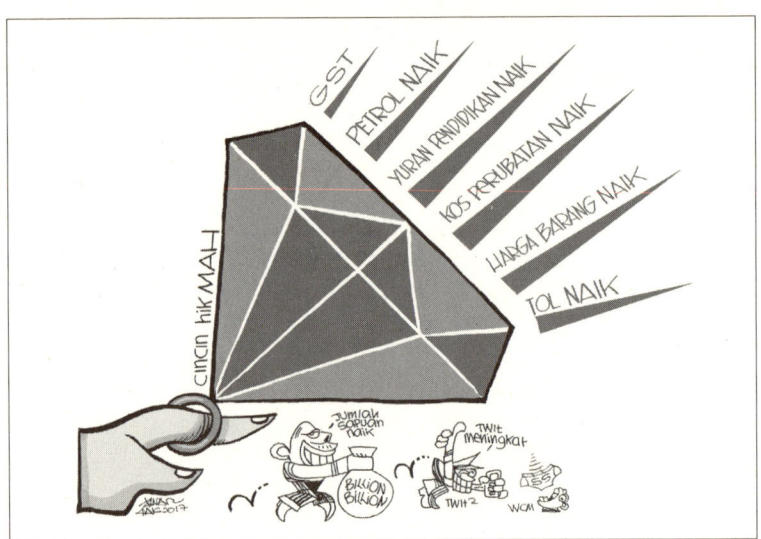

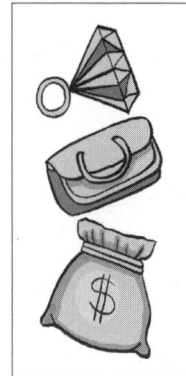  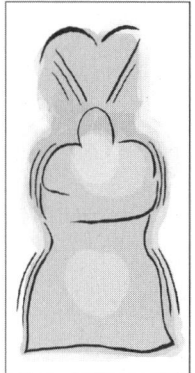 

The first attempt to launch *Ros in Kangkong Land* was disrupted by the police and as a result, many of my fans could not buy the book.

The police blocked the venue for the second attempt to launch *Ros in Kangkong Land* in Brickfields.

The police on standby to make sure *Ros in Kangkong Land* does not get launched.

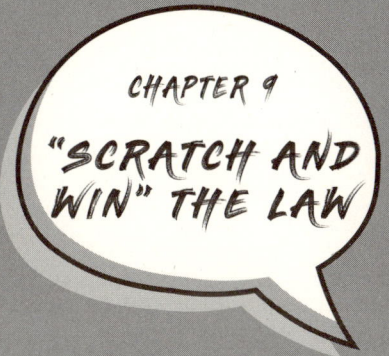

CHAPTER 9

"SCRATCH AND WIN" THE LAW

"SCRATCH AND WIN" THE LAW
Funny and spicy cartoons

SINCE MY CARTOONS HIGHLIGHTED ISSUES such as corruption, I needed to find a way to make them comfortable and enjoyable for the people.

So in terms of visuals, I needed to come up with a concept that could cater to people of every age group, from children to the elders, and every social class, from kampung folk to professionals. I came up with the idea of having a side cartoon next to the main cartoon.

When I draw a main cartoon, it would normally show two or more characters say, for example, taking money from the people, as well as details such as the amount of money. But by itself, young people may not understand what this means. The same goes for the apolitical or those who don't know much about the issue. So I would create a side cartoon for them which has its own story. This cartoon is normally very small and appears only in black and white form.

From feedback, I learnt that some people read the small cartoon first and then go on to the main cartoon. While others would read the main cartoon first, before going for the small details. For me, either would be fine. The important thing is to get them interested to read my cartoons and get the message at the end of the day.

Another funny step I took concerned the names of printers in my books. After three printers were raided by the authorities, many printers were afraid to print my books. This was due to the requirement by law to state the printer's name on the third page of a book, but if this requirement was complied with, the police would pay the printer a visit. So finally, there were no printers who dared to print my books. I had to find a solution for this and, at the same time, make fun of the law.

Finally, I found a way. I blackened the name of the printer. On top of it, I put a note to the police: "If you want to know who the printer is, please enter scratch-and-win contest."

I did not want to do this, but I had no choice. The Printing Presses and Publications Act (PPPA) is supposed to protect the author and not be used as a weapon to threaten them.

In another book, *Wasabi*, I began making fun of the book's price tag. In Malaysia during that time, the popular issue was the RM2.6 billion (US$681 million) Najib had received in his private bank account which he claimed was a donation. I began selling my books at RM26. It was my way to remind people about the corruption in Malaysia. So when my readers looked at the price tag, they could see just how big the corruption was.

In my latest cartoon book, *Ketawa Pink Pink*, I began poking fun at the International Standard Book Number (ISBN). Instead of ISBN, I changed it to ISPH. In Malaysia, BN is short form for the then ruling party, Barisan Nasional. So ISBN to me could be humorously interpreted as "I Support Barisan Nasional". Instead of that, why not change it to ISPH, which could mean "I Support Pakatan Harapan". Pakatan Harapan was the Opposition during that time.

Also, in *Lawak & Lawan*, I made fun of the barcode. Instead of using a normal barcode, I changed the barcode to prison bars and drew Najib, Rosmah and Mahathir in jail.

I once drew a man's underwear on which was written "S.S.", which appeared in a small corner of many of my cartoons. "S.S." meant "Spender Saiful" (Saiful's underwear). That underwear represents the underwear the police had used as evidence in the conspiracy to put Anwar in jail.

I also drew a small character, "WCM", which means, "Wa Cari Makan" (I'm trying to make a living). This was to mock a top civil servant who compromised his principles and work ethics to blindly support a ruling party in return for a reward.

By doing all this, I created dimension and added layers to my cartoons. If you look at the cartoons, the main focus is on serious issues with strong political messages. Sometimes, they could be less humorous. In creating dimension, I hoped to cater to both segments of the public. Those who were aware of Malaysian politics would read the main cartoon first and then look out for the other details.

For the others, they might look at the small characters first, after which they would look at the main cartoon. The purpose of doing this was to make those who were apolitical feel comfortable to read my cartoons. It was like selecting a dish where there was an option of either a main course or a dessert. Whether you chose a main course or a dessert, I, as the chef, would be very happy.

I changed the price of my cartoon books to RM26 as a reminder to people about the RM2.6 billion 1MDB corruption scandal.

Even the letters in ISBN were changed to ISPH. Satirically, ISBN is "I Support Barisan Nasional" and ISPH is "I Support Pakatan Harapan".

In another book, the barcode was turned into prison bars for corrupt leaders.

The title for my latest book *Wasabi* is short for "Wa Sapu Billion" (I Steal Billions).

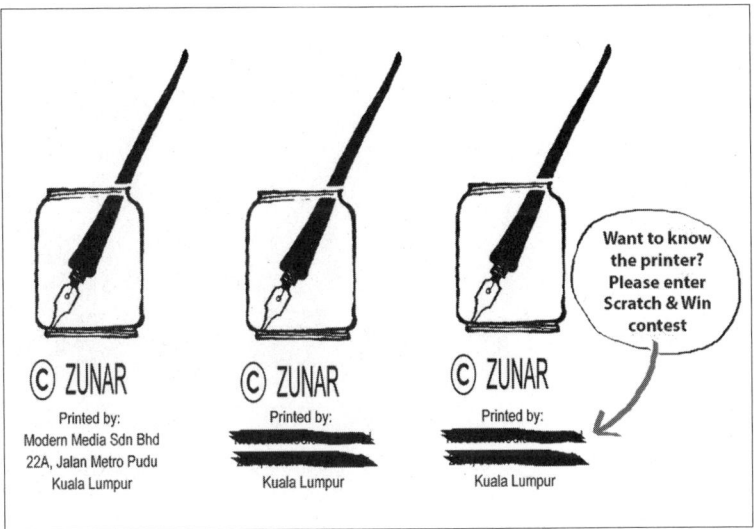

| The law requires the name of the printer to be printed on the third page of the book. | After the raids, printers became frightened to have their names printed. So I had to blacken their names. | This was my message to the police if they wanted to know who the printers were. |

The drawing of this underwear appears in my cartoons regularly as a symbol of the political conspiracy against Anwar Ibrahim.

Twit Twit represents the police chief who uses Twitter to arrest people. The price tag on the hair is a representation of the lavish spending of the prime minister's wife.

WCM represents civil servants who blindly support the corrupt. The (yellow) balloon on the other hand symbolises Malaysians who oppose corruption.

TWIT, TWIT
Nights in police lock-up

MEANWHILE, IN THE POLITICAL ARENA, Anwar Ibrahim was arrested and put on trial again. This was the second time he was falsely charged with sodomy through a political conspiracy. When I met him briefly during the previous trial, I had told him that their motive was to send him to jail and the legal process was just a formality.

On February 10, 2015, all Malaysians waited nervously for the decision on Anwar's case. At the Palace of Justice in Putrajaya, five judges were ready to deliver their verdict. I was at home, following the process closely. Before the judgment was delivered, I had already prepared one cartoon and a few captions for publication after the decision was delivered. I knew precisely what the outcome would be.

As I had expected, the five judges made the decision to send Anwar to jail for five years, up to June 2020, which meant Anwar would be released in June 2018 after deducting public holidays. It was a normal process for prisoners.

This sentence was to prevent Anwar from taking part in the general elections which had to be held before June 2018. Immediately after the judgment was delivered, I released some tweets and the cartoons which I had prepared earlier.

One of the tweets read, "Barua2 berjubah hitam bangga jatuhkan hukuman. Habuan dari tuan politik pasti lumayan" (The lackeys in black robes are proud of their sentence. The reward from their political masters must be plenty). When I tweeted this, the government became very sensitive. As far as I was concerned, if they had delivered a good judgment, why were they sensitive? When I said that this was scripted, they were angry.

At around 3pm, the then Inspector General of Police Khalid Abu Bakar retweeted my tweet and instructed the police to arrest me. He did all of this through Twitter.

At around 9pm that night, some six to seven policemen were at the gate of my house. My wife alerted me to this and when I looked out the window, I knew they were here for me. I went down to see them at the gate and they told me that they were going to arrest me. I told the police to wait for a while because I needed to shower and pack my medication. But this was a tactic I used in order to inform the journalists to report on my arrest. I called Malaysiakini editor, Fathi Aris Omar, to inform them about the arrest. He immediately updated the incident on the web portal.

After taking a small bag of medication, I went to the gate. The police were ready to arrest me. I was handcuffed and put into the car with three other policemen. They drove me to Dang Wangi Police Station. At the station, the police also confiscated my handphone. After that, they brought me to the changing room where I had to take off all my clothes and shoes. They gave me nothing but an orange pair of shorts and a t-shirt, and I was left barefooted. One of the officers recorded all the items that were taken from me, such as my wallet, the money inside, my keys and shirt. I was then brought to a cell and the prison bars were slammed and locked. I then realised that there were 12 other inmates in the cell. I was quite afraid to see them because of their scary faces but I took the friendly approach and chatted with them. Later on, I discovered that they were arrested for robbery, drugs and other forms of crime. There were, however, some who were wrongly arrested.

The lock-up was made of steel bars and there were many connected rooms. The officers who were stationed outside the cell could see what was happening inside. On top of that, they had CCTV to monitor our activities in the cells. The cement floor had an uneven surface. There was also a wooden plank for sleeping on but no mattress or pillows. The toilet was of the open air type, so when you went to the toilet, everybody could see. There was no towel. So when you wanted to take a bath, you had to do it with your clothes on and wait for your body and clothes to dry.

To make matters worse, I couldn't sleep the whole night until the next morning. Around me, there was only wood, steel and cement. By 2am, the others were already sleeping on the wooden plank but I couldn't do that because I have a vertigo problem that prevents me from sleeping on a flat surface. So I sat there, leaning against the steel bar the whole night. At 6am, I heard a voice calling, "Hi Zunar!" When I turned to look, it was a policeman. He had just come in for the morning shift. He looked like he recognised me. He approached me and offered me his hand to shake, which I accepted. "Why did you wake up so early?" he asked. I said I couldn't sleep because of my vertigo. I then explained to him what it was. He went away and came back with a few lock-up shirts. "This is your pillow," he said, and I replied, "Thank you for the much needed assistance."

I was then able to take a short nap before the place became noisy. I could hear people shouting, and it was breakfast time.

I was served a small slice of bread with extremely diluted tea. This was the type of food we were served. For lunch, it was a tiny portion of rice with very diluted curry and a small piece of fish. It was the same for dinner, which was served at 6pm. Nothing more was served after that. When I was released later, I had lost 5kg. I think this is the best free-of-charge weight loss scheme and after that I continued with this lock-up diet because it works.

After breakfast at 8am, it was court proceedings time. The names of the inmates were called one by one by the police who came in for their cases. They were brought to court to settle their remand orders. At about 9am, the Investigation Officer called me and I was handcuffed and brought to another room where I saw my lawyer, Melissa Sasidaran, waiting for me. After a discussion with her, I was brought to another room for my remand proceeding. The magistrate was there. The proceeding began with arguments from my lawyer and at the end, the court granted three days of remand detention.

Later, I was brought for interrogation under the Sedition Act. Melissa had advised me earlier that I had the right not to answer any questions except those on my personal particulars. After two hours, the interrogation was done, and I was brought back to the lock-up.

The next morning, I was transferred from Dang Wangi Police Station to Bukit Aman Police Headquarters for another round of investigations and taking of statements. Somehow, my supporters had found out about the transfer and had gathered outside the station. I don't know who had told them but I was shocked to see so many of my fans. When I was brought out, some of them took pictures but stopped when they were scolded by the police.

After 15 minutes, I arrived at Bukit Aman. They took me to the 10th floor and there I saw seven police personnel monitoring Facebook and Twitter. One of the officers said that my Facebook was among their top targets. When he showed me my Facebook page, I was shocked to see that the photo of my transfer to Bukit Aman was already there.

He asked me, "How come so fast?" I replied, "I don't know. I don't even have access to the page."

The Bukit Aman investigation was for intelligence interrogation. I had to provide to the police my personal information, including details of the schools and tertiary institutions I had attended, my friends and whether I was involved in any activities related to politics. I also had to provide details about my parents, siblings and my wife.

That afternoon, I was brought back to Dang Wangi Police Station where a few police officers were waiting. One of them introduced himself as an ASP from the Kuala Lumpur headquarters police contingent. He said I had to give another statement for a different case. This case was related to the publication of my cartoon books. After that, I was brought to another room for photo-taking and documentation. The police took my picture with my prisoner's number. They also took fingerprints of all my fingers.

The next afternoon, I was released. I then made a statement referring to IGP Khalid who had used Twitter to order my arrest. I said that starting that day, I would draw him every day in my cartoons holding a handphone and tweeting.

That was how "Twit, Twit" came about. From then on, his tiny character appeared in the corner of my cartoons which were published daily. This was my way of using cartoons and laughter to fight tyranny.

People started to respond and laugh when they discovered that the Twit, Twit cartoon was in reference to this incident. According to them, they looked forward to my cartoons every day, partly because they wanted to know what Twit, Twit was up to.

When I was in Los Angeles on a speaking tour, many fans had asked what Twit, Twit meant, and when I explained the history behind it, they were so amused. They responded generously by purchasing many of my books. During the autograph session, many of them were willing to pay an extra $10 for me to draw the character of Twit, Twit next to my signature.

I didn't know how IGP Khalid reacted to it. But I found out during the month of Ramadhan in June 2016 when I was on a five-city tour of Australia which included Sydney, Adelaide, Canberra, Melbourne and Perth. When I was in Sydney, I went to a well-known restaurant which served authentic Malay food to "*buka puasa*" (break my fast). The owner of the restaurant was very proud to receive me.

A week later, when I was in Melbourne, I learnt that IGP Khalid had arrived in Sydney and visited the same restaurant to *buka puasa*. According to a source, the owner of the restaurant was very happy to see another famous Malaysian visiting his restaurant. He told IGP Khalid that many well-known Malaysians had come to his restaurant, including the prime minister and his wife. Then he added that even the cartoonist Zunar was there the previous week.

Upon hearing this, according to the WhatsApp text I received, IGP Khalid became very angry and complained loudly about me making fun of him in my cartoons.

On December 2, 2016, IGP Khalid was in Penang for an official function. That was a week after I was arrested in Penang for another case. After the function, there was a press conference. During the press conference, Malaysiakini reporter Susan Loone had asked him why I was arrested earlier. IGP Khalid said it was because I had drawn bad cartoons about the prime minister and his wife.

Susan then responded by asking, as a political cartoonist, what should Zunar draw? IGP Khalid said I should draw Donald Duck.

The next day, I was sitting at my table scratching my head for ideas and didn't know what to draw. I switched on my laptop to read Malaysiakini and I saw the news article headlined "IGP tells Zunar to draw Donald Duck instead of insulting leaders".

I thought, thank you, Khalid, for the brilliant idea. I grabbed my pen and started drawing. I drew the prime minister as Donald Duck carrying a big sack of money while his wife, as Mickey Mouse, waited to receive the money.

I changed Donald Duck to Donald Dedak. "Dedak" in Malay means "chicken feed". It is a famous word referring to Najib's way of using money to buy support. In that cartoon, Mickey Mouse was known as Mickey Mah. Mah is my cartoon word for Rosmah.

The cartoon was a hit and became a hot topic during that period. There were requests from some fans to buy the original version of the cartoon with a high price offer, but I refused to sell. Following the publication of this cartoon, I was arrested again.

This didn't stop me from drawing Twit, Twit. I continued to do so until IGP Khalid retired on September 4, 2017. I even used the phrase Twit, Twit as the title of one of my cartoon books later on.

A news clipping on the jailing of Anwar Ibrahim by The Washington Post.

The Inspector General of Police (IGP) Khalid Abu Bakar ordered my arrest through a Twitter posting.

Following Anwar Ibrahim's jail sentence, I had posted: "The lackeys in black robes are proud of their sentence. The reward from their political masters must be plenty."

The IGP then posted a screenshot of my tweet and said, "This person has also invited police action. Police Cyber Investigation Response Centre (PCIRC) please trace and investigate."

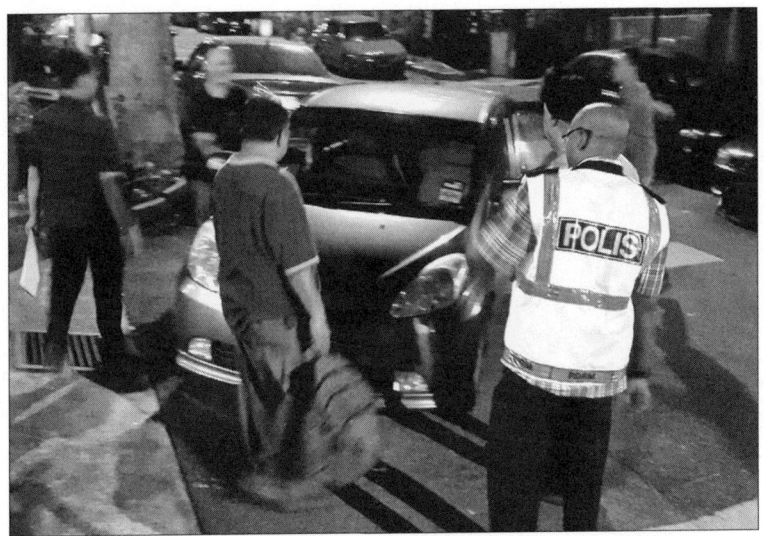
The police arrived at my house at around 9pm to arrest me on February 10, 2015.

This picture by my lawyer was taken before
the remand procedure at Dang Wangi Police Station.

On the second day, I was transferred to the Bukit Aman Police Headquarters for intelligence interrogation.

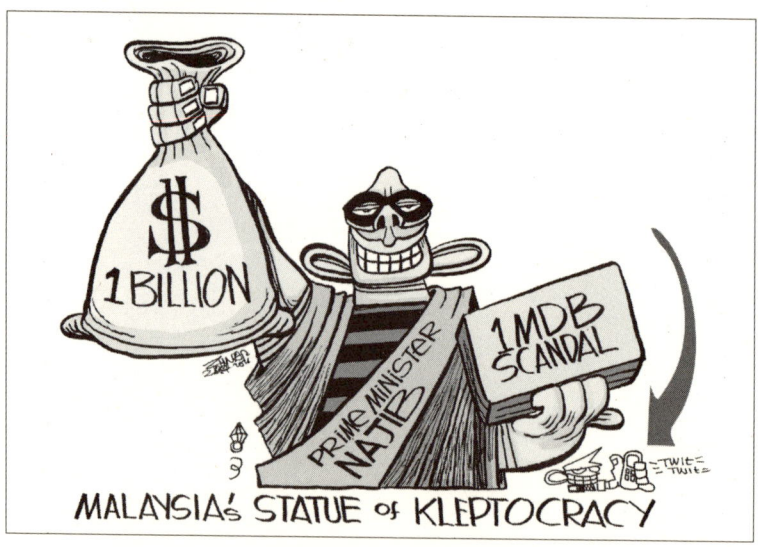

Following my release, I began drawing IGP Khalid every day in my cartoons, holding a smartphone and tweeting. I drew him for more than 900 days until he retired in September 2017.

He appears at the corner of my cartoons regardless of the issue.

Again.

And again.

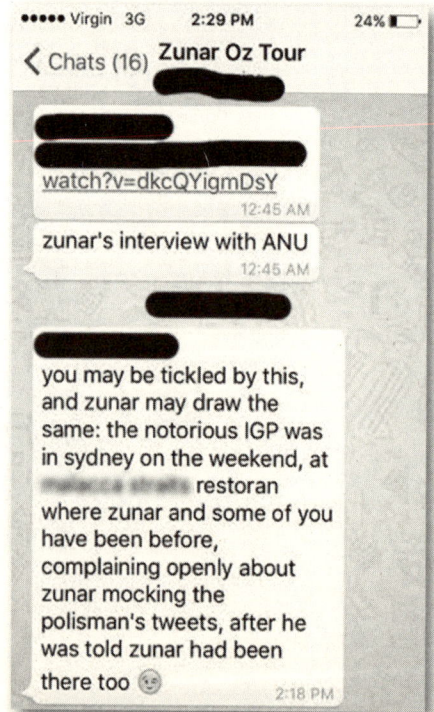

I never knew what Khalid Abu Bakar's reaction to my cartoons was until I read this WhatsApp message from a friend.

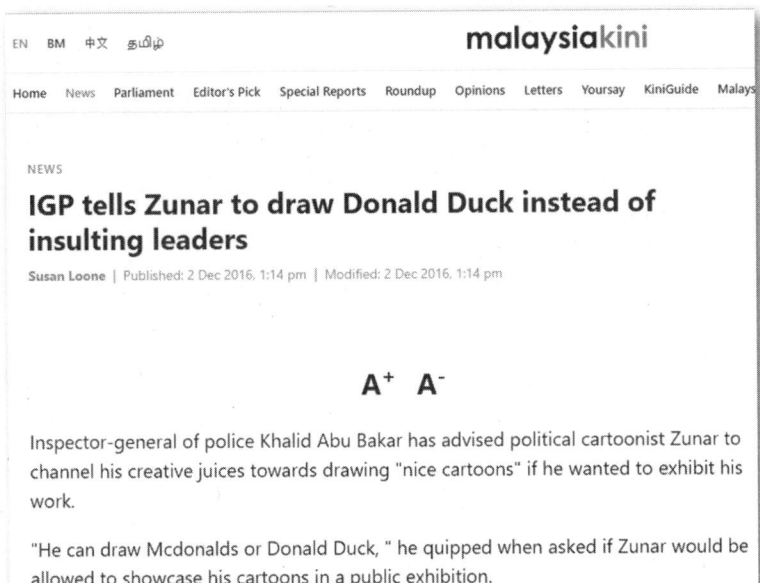

When asked by reporters on what should Zunar draw, this is what IGP Khalid said.

That's a great idea, IGP Khalid. I will use it.

As an obedient citizen, I followed IGP Khalid's instruction. On December 5, 2016, I came out with this cartoon, "Donald Dedak & Mickey MAH". I was arrested again a week later for being detrimental to Parliamentary Democracy.

Donald Dedak became a constant feature at that time.

The cover for *Twit Twit Cin Cin*.

CHAPTER 11
WHICH IS BIGGER, FEAR OR RESPONSIBILITY?

WHICH IS BIGGER, FEAR OR RESPONSIBILITY?
Nine sedition charges, 43 years' jail

A FEW WEEKS AFTER MY release from Dang Wangi police lock-up, I received a call from my lawyer, Latheefa Koya, who told me that the police had informed her that they would charge me under the Sedition Act at the Sessions Court in Kuala Lumpur on April 1, 2015. The police had also advised me to prepare RM5,000 (US$1,192) for bail money. Under the Malaysian legal system, bail money is required pending trial when someone is brought to court, otherwise the person will go straight to jail.

I considered RM5,000 as manageable. But the day before I was brought to court, the police came back and informed me that there would be nine charges under the Sedition Act, for which I needed to prepare RM45,000 (US$10,732) for bail money. This amount of money was too much for me and it was impossible to obtain this amount in ten hours. So I panicked.

The only way to raise the funds was to make this known to the Malaysian public. I posted a plea on Twitter and Facebook. The post read: "Dear Malaysians, tomorrow I'll be charged with nine charges for sedition and I need RM45,000 for bail money. Here is my bank account, please support me." That post was widely circulated. I received many pledges and inquiries from every part of Malaysia, and even from overseas such as London and Geneva. People began to deposit money into my account.

I also felt that I needed to create a gimmick for the media. I called up my good friend, Tham, who was a small-time shirt manufacturer. I asked if he could create a lock-up attire and a replica of a pair of handcuffs, similar to the one that I wore when I was arrested. It was a last-minute plan and request, but Tham managed to get it done and delivered to me.

The next day at 7.30am, I arrived at the Kuala Lumpur Court Complex in Jalan Duta. I went to the ground floor to have my breakfast. Already there were several lawyers including former Bar Council president, Ambiga Sreenevasan, and Latheefa Koya who would represent me.

I wore the lock-up attire and brought the handcuffs. I was very surprised to see so many reporters and journalists waiting, around 30 to 40 of them, from local and international media. When they saw me with the purple lock-up shirt and pants and handcuffs, the photographers asked me to pose for their cameras.

Then people started to arrive, including Datuk Seri Wan Azizah, the wife of Anwar Ibrahim. By 9am, together with my lawyers, a group of supporters followed by journalists, I went to the Sessions Court.

When the trial started, I was asked to sit in the dock and the Deputy Public Prosecutor (DPP) who was representing the Malaysian government read out the nine charges against me. I pleaded not guilty. The DPP asked the court to impose RM45,000 (US$11,000) bail on me. But Judge Zanol Rashid Hussain reduced my bail to RM22,000 (US$5,500) after arguments from my lawyers. The bail could not be processed immediately as it was then lunch hour on a Friday. The police put me in the court lock-up, which was located deep underground.

When I was in the lock-up, I noticed a female police officer walking by who appeared to be looking for someone. I recognised her face but couldn't recall her name. After asking around, she came to my cell and asked me to come closer to the bars. I saw her name tag and realised she was ASP Sutha, who had investigated me earlier.

I asked her why she was there and she replied that she was there to arrest me. I said I had already paid my bail and was waiting to be released, but she said it was for another offence.

This was their tactic to keep me locked up. Nine charges were not enough to really silence me. They had added one more. After six hours, a police officer came over to me, opened the lock-up door and arrested me again.

I was brought upstairs to see my lawyers and a few supporters. There was a slight argument as my lawyers were very angry that the police had arrested me again. My lawyers asked the police officer where they wanted to bring me. He said to Dang Wangi Police Station. After a long argument, my supporters said that at the very least, I should be given a chance to have my lunch first. Luckily, the police agreed and someone brought *nasi bungkus* for me.

While having my lunch, I whispered to my assistant Yong to keep my phone because I knew they would confiscate it, based on my previous experience. I asked her to go back to my house and get my old "*cap ayam*" (cheap) phone and bring that to me instead.

After I had finished eating, I was brought to the police car and taken to the police station. Malaysiakini ran the news, "Zunar arrested again after posting bail".

I was brought to Dang Wangi Police Station. ASP Sutha handed me over to ASP Liew for investigation. He told me that he was going to confiscate my phone. I told him that I didn't bring my handphone. He asked, "How come?" I replied that the police had already confiscated my phone earlier. I didn't have a phone except an old phone. "I can call someone to bring it if you want it," I said to him.

He then handed me his phone to call Yong. I told Yong discreetly to change the SIM card in the old phone and to bring the phone to the police station.

Half an hour or so later, Yong called and informed me that she couldn't change the SIM card because the card slot was different. I told her to go to the nearest shopping complex and buy a cheap phone that could fit the card. When the phone arrived, I surrendered it to ASP Liew.

Then the investigation started. It was about an image on my Facebook. According to the police, I had posted an image of the prime minister of Malaysia. The edited photo showed my lock-up attire and handcuffs, but the face had been changed to Najib's face. It was uploaded onto my Facebook page. The police wanted to know if I did it. I said no, this was very amateur. I never used photos in my art and if I wanted to create an image, I would draw it. So this was definitely not my doing.

He asked if I was the one who uploaded it. I said no, I was busy the past few days handling my charges and was in the lock-up, I had no time to do this.

Then he said this was uploaded to my Facebook page. I said it was not by me. Maybe it was one of the administrators. Then he asked me to name my administrators. I told him I had 500 administrators and couldn't name them all. He knew I was not telling the truth, but he couldn't do anything about it. In my view, cheating an oppressive regime is not a crime.

After four hours, I was released on police bail. This became big news internationally. The photo of me in handcuffs was widely circulated by newspapers and news portals around the world. An international photographer told me later that he had only three individuals in Malaysia who were saleable around the world: prime minister Najib, opposition leader Anwar Ibrahim and me.

The charges against me were condemned by various governments and international organisations. They sent a letter to Najib, demanding the nine sedition charges against me to be dropped. The organisations were Amnesty International, Human Rights Watch, Article 19, English PEN, Index on Censorship, Media Legal Defence Initiative and PEN International.

"Freedom of expression is an essential part of any democratic society and the Malaysian authorities must protect this right for all, including those who are critical of government," one of the paragraphs in the letter read.

UN Special Rapporteur for cultural rights, Karima Bennoune, said the Sedition Act should be abolished as per Najib's promise. Even the US government urged the Malaysian government to drop the sedition charges against me. Locally, Suara Rakyat Malaysia (Suaram) called for the Sedition Act to be abolished.

On September 16, 2015, I received the International Press Freedom Award by the Committee to Protect Journalists (CPJ) in New York. I was the first cartoonist to receive this award. It was presented to me by famous international cartoonist, Garry Trudeau, who created the Doonesbury comic strip. I was also invited to speak at the United Nations and Amnesty International in London. The School of Oriental & African Studies (SOAS) in London also invited me to speak.

During this time, I was also chosen as one of the ten individual world icons for the Write for Rights (#W4R) campaign organised by Amnesty International. I was the first Malaysian and first cartoonist to be selected. Through this campaign, I received 250,000 letters and postcards from around the world. I also received many pieces of solidarity art from artists around the world, including Harry Belafonte and Ai Weiwei.

Why nine sedition charges and not one? With one charge, I could get away on a technicality, but with nine charges, I didn't stand much of a chance.

A judge could acquit me of seven of the nine charges. Two charges could land me in prison for six years. This was their tactic to get me in jail.

People asked me if I have any fear. I said yes, I have fear like you, because I am human. I am just someone who wants to perform my duties, but then it comes to the question of which is bigger — fear or responsibility?

During a question and answer session in one of my talks, someone remarked, "You must have many balls ..." I replied, "No, only two like you."

During an interview by *The Guardian* at the newspaper's headquarters in King's Place, London, the journalist asked a similar question. She asked why I didn't apply for political asylum in Britain? I replied, "No, I want to go back."

She asked me why I wanted to do such a thing. I said the issue was not about me: if I applied for political asylum, it might save me from 43 years in jail, but it wouldn't save my country. The corruption issues were still rife and the government would be very happy if I ran away.

I told her I want to go back and use my case to create awareness during the trial. I said that we have to fight. If we didn't fight, we would lose. But if we fought, we would have two possible outcomes. Either I would end up in jail or Najib would end up in jail.

At the time of writing this book, Najib is facing charges for corruption.

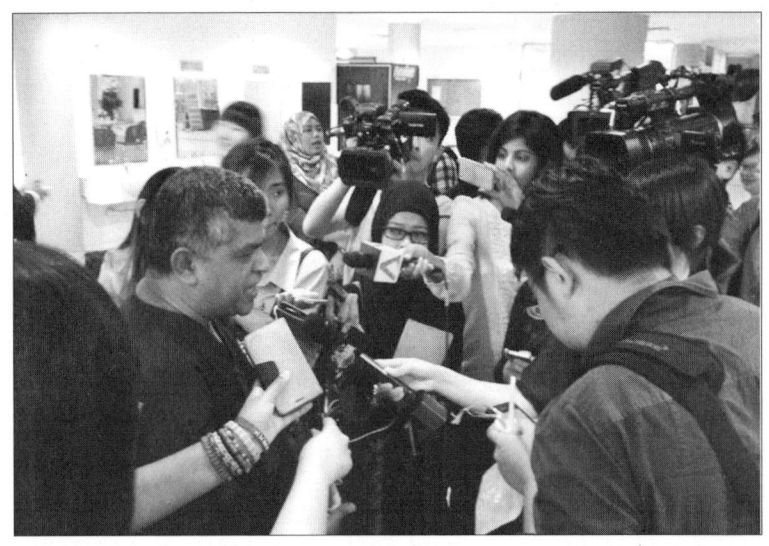

I am surrounded by local and international reporters at the Kuala Lumpur High Court, where I was charged for nine counts under the Sedition Act.

Which is Bigger, Fear or Responsibility? 163

I faced 43 years in prison if found guilty under
the Sedition Act for my tweets and cartoons.

Walking to the courtroom with my lawyers Ambiga Sreenevasan
and Latheefa Koya to face the nine sedition charges.

This iconic image was circulated around the world.

I am in the courtroom waiting for my case to be heard.

Which is Bigger, Fear or Responsibility? 165

International cartoonists show their support for me by holding a protest in front of the Malaysian embassy in Washington DC.

Because of my tight schedule, I had to conduct interviews with international media in the car.

Malaysians living in London show their support for me outside 10 Downing Street.

Conducting a cartoon demonstration at Washington Square, New York.

I explained my case to the international audience at the Cartooning for Peace event at Le Dessin in Paris.

I was invited to be one of the panelists at a United Nation's forum titled "Defending Artistic Expression – Time For The UN To Act".

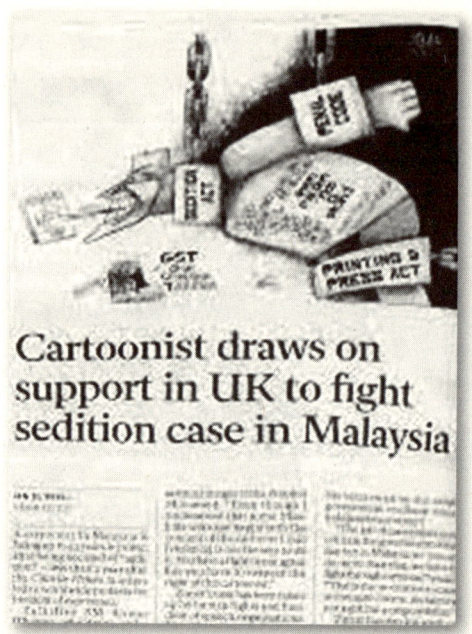

A news clipping from *The Independent* — October 27, 2015.

Students at the University of Oxford listen intently as I speak to them about my struggle.

I will keep drawing until the last drop of my ink, says Malaysian cartoonist

KUALA LUMPUR — Malaysian political cartoonist Zunar faces a possible 43 years in prison for sedition, but the defiant artist says that looming threat won't stop his hard-hitting caricatures lampooning the ruling establishment.

"You can chain my hands, you can chain my legs, you can chain my neck or my body. But I will keep drawing," said Zunar, 52, holding a cartoon showing himself shackled yet still working with a pen clenched in his teeth.

"I will keep drawing until the last drop of my ink," he added during an interview at his Kuala Lumpur office.

Malaysia's best-known political cartoonist, whose real name is Zulkiflee Anwar Ulhaque, has become a symbol of a widening government drive to throttle its critics that has seen dozens of people hit with sedition investigations over the past year.

Zunar has been arrested previously and his works, which skewer the government's recurring corruption scandals and alleged repression, have repeatedly been seized by police in what he calls a "political vendetta".

But the pressure escalated dramatically on April 3 with the filing of nine sedition charges — a single-day Malaysian "record", according to his lawyers.

They could potentially land Zunar in jail for 43 years, his lawyers say, though the penalty is not expected to be that harsh.

Few have actually been jailed in the sedition blitz, which political analysts view more as a bid by the 58-year-old government to cow and silence adversaries as it loses ground to a reform-minded opposition. — *AFP*

Cartoonist Zunar

A news clipping from a United Arab Emirates daily.

I received 250,000 letters of support from fans across the globe through the Write for Rights (#W4R) campaign organised by Amnesty International.

Speaking to participants at a talk organised by Amnesty International in London.

Demonstration in front of Tourism Malaysia office in London with *Sarawak Report* editor, Clare Rewcastle Brown.

I presented my case to Germany's Federal Government Commissioner for Human Rights Policy and Humanitarian Aid, Bärbel Kofler, who met with me in Berlin.

My book ban and arrests attracted the attention of the Indonesian media.

PRISONER IN HOMELAND
Meeting Kofi Annan in Geneva

AFTER YEARS OF HARASSMENT, book bans, office raids, raids on printers, charges, detentions, arrests and attempts at intimidation against me, I thought I had faced it all, but I was wrong.

On October 17, 2016, I was at the Kuala Lumpur International Airport (KLIA) to board a flight to Singapore. I had an invitation to speak with students at the National University in Singapore. When I arrived at the immigration counter, I was told by an immigration officer that my name was on the blacklist. The officer apologised and said that I could not board the flight. I asked the officer for the reason I was on the blacklist, but she said she could not give me the details as this was an instruction from the government. I took a selfie with her holding my passport.

Usually, when a person receives a travel ban, there is a reason for it, and it is commonly imposed on Malaysians who have failed to pay their education loans.

I had already checked in my luggage, so I had to hurry quickly to retrieve the bags. When I got them back, I quickly uploaded the photo of me at the immigration counter on social media with the caption that I was stopped from travelling abroad.

At the same time, I called a contact from the Immigration Department on this matter. He went through my records and said the ban was because of special reasons. My contact also said that the travel ban was imposed a few months earlier on June 24.

I suspected the travel ban was imposed because of my exhibition in Geneva, Switzerland, held in May. It was officiated by the former Secretary General of the United Nations, the late Kofi Annan. Also present were well-known political cartoonist, Plantu, and the mayor of Geneva.

The exhibition was held at Lac Léman (Lake Geneva), Geneva, near the United Nations building. It is a popular spot for the public to go to jogging, walking and cycling. I had exhibited 20 works. The size of the exhibition was as big as a billboard.

My cartoons touched mainly on the 1Malaysia Development Berhad (1MDB) scandal. During the exhibition tour, I explained to Kofi Annan about the amount of RM2.6 billion (US$681 million) which had gone into the Malaysian prime minister's bank account. Kofi Annan replied, "They said it was a donation, wasn't it?" This showed that he knew what was happening and was monitoring the situation.

Some of the cartoons also focused on Najib and how he had transferred the powers of the military to himself through the National Security Council Act. This law was passed in Parliament on February 18, 2016.

The exhibition was part of the recognition given by the organiser, Cartooning for Peace Foundation, to award recipients. Earlier, another cartoonist from Kenya, Gado, and I had received the Cartooning for Peace award, which was conferred by Kofi Annan on May 3, 2016, which coincided with World Press Freedom Day.

The award conferment was held at Palais Eynard, Geneva. During the speech, Kofi Annan said, "Zunar reminds us how fragile this liberty remains in Africa and in Asia, as well as in other regions of the world. Through his commitment towards open and transparent societies, Zunar, who has received threats in his country of origin and can no longer practice his profession, confronts us with our responsibility to preserve freedom of expression and act in order to support the combat of those who cannot express themselves through their art."

I also had the opportunity to meet Kofi Annan separately and privately at his office. During the meeting, I explained to him the situation in Malaysia and also about the jailing of opposition leader, Anwar Ibrahim. Prior to the meeting, I had managed to get a letter from Anwar, who was in prison, to be given to Kofi Annan.

The exhibition in Geneva became popular among the locals because of the lake's destination as a leisure spot. Some of them stopped to ask me about the cartoons and the issues related to them.

I suspected this angered the Malaysian government and led to the travel ban. During that time, a few senior ministers openly condemned the exhibition. First was the Communications and Multimedia Minister, Salleh Said Keruak, who said I had sabotaged the Malaysian economy through my exhibition.

I replied to him point by point, saying that I was not responsible. The government was corrupt and it was him and the others in power who had sabotaged the Malaysian economy. Having stolen billions, they then blamed cartoonists for the economic problem. How could they blame cartoonists?

What had caught my attention, however, were his use of the words "sabotage Malaysian economy". Previously, one of the 1MDB critics was accused of sabotaging the Malaysian economy and he was charged under section 124L of the Penal Code, which allowed the government to detain him without trial. At that point, I was worried that it would also be used against me.

Then, it was the Deputy Prime Minister Zahid Hamidi's turn to condemn the exhibition. Zahid at that time was also the Home Minister who was in charge of the police. He said my cartoons were disrespectful and that he was leaving the matter to the police. When a Home Minister says he leaves a matter to the police, it can be interpreted as an instruction to the police.

This was how I suspected the travel ban was initiated. There was even a group of Umno supporters who announced on national television that they were going to protest in front of Kofi Annan's office because of my exhibition.

The legal condition of my travel ban was worse than that of the other activists. The head of Bersih, Maria Chin Abdullah, and then Opposition politician Tony Pua were also banned from travelling. But the period of their ban was temporary while mine was indefinite.

During this time, IGP Khalid in a media statement invited me to go to Bukit Aman to discuss the travel ban but I declined, as I knew it would not be a normal discussion. I knew that if I were to go there, the police would put many conditions and restrictions on me, and even arrest me. So, instead, on December 7, 2016, I went to the courts to challenge the legality of the travel ban, and I named the Home Ministry, the police and the Immigration Department as the respondents. According to the law, my rights under Article 5 (right to life), Article 8 (right to equality) and Article 9 (right to movement) of the Constitution had been breached.

My travel ban became an international issue because it was mind-boggling to ban a cartoonist from leaving his home country. I received support from international organisations from all over the world who had sent a letter demanding Najib to lift the ban. They were Cartoonists Rights Network International (CRNI), Cartooning for Peace Foundation, Cartoon Movement, Comic Book Legal Defence Fund, Committee to Protect Journalists, International Federation of Journalists and Wikipedia's co-founder, Jimmy Wales.

> We join the International and Human Rights NGOs and call upon Malaysian authorities to lift the travel ban on Zunar with immediate effect and to drop the numerous sedition charges against him. We pay tribute to Zunar and other editorial cartoonists for their courage to work and draw under very difficult circumstances in many regions of the world.

A few months after that, I was invited to go to Kenya to speak at the Satire Festival in conjunction with World Press Freedom Day on May 4, 2017. I replied to the invitation letter, saying that I couldn't attend because I was under a travel ban. The organiser from Kenya replied that he was shocked by this. He said Africa was bad, but he didn't know it was worse in Malaysia.

Prior to the travel ban, one of the organisers at Morges, Switzerland, had invited me to do an exhibition in a museum called Maison du Design de Presse. This was the first time I had the opportunity to exhibit my works in a museum and it took six months to curate. The launch and opening was planned for January 26, 2017, and I was invited to speak at the event as an artist but by this time I couldn't travel. As it was so important for me to attend, I applied to the Immigration Department to allow me to travel temporarily, but they didn't respond to my letter of request.

I had also received an invitation by Amnesty International to speak in Sydney and an invitation from London to speak at the IFEX (formerly International Freedom of Expression Exchange) event. For both occasions, I once again wrote letters to the Immigration Department to release me temporarily to travel to the events. Finally, they replied, saying that as this was a police case, I needed to get permission from Bukit Aman instead, but the police, as expected, didn't reply.

When the United Nations (UN) Special Rapporteur, Karima Bennoune, visited Malaysia in September 2017, she met me and other activists in private. After the meeting, she wanted to meet me separately and wanted a report from me on my case. During our meeting, I told her that I was not satisfied with the UN because whenever their representatives came, they collected reports and quietly gave them to the Malaysian government.

I explained to her that the Malaysian government did not care or bother about this method of handling matters. If the UN presented a complaint quietly, that was exactly what the government wanted. I told her that if the UN was serious about my case, they would make it public and immediate. It would then put pressure on the government.

I said if she really wanted to help me, she had to issue a statement openly while she was in Malaysia. She did it on September 21, 2017. In her statement, Karima urged the Malaysian government to immediately drop my nine sedition charges and lift my travel ban.

On January 21, 2017, one of my cartoons appeared again in Switzerland. This time, it was featured on the big screen during a discussion at the World Economic Forum in Davos. The cartoon in the first panel showed Donald Trump with the caption, "Billionaire becomes a president". The second panel depicted Najib with the caption, "The prime minister becomes a billionaire".

It was a big achievement for me because this is the most prestigious economic forum in the world. It is attended by top business and world leaders, celebrities, economists and the international media.

Meanwhile, on November 29, 2017, I went to the High Court for the judgment on the status of my travel ban. The outcome was negative. The High Court judge, Azizah Nawawi, rejected my challenge and said the travel ban would remain. She also said the government had the absolute right to stop citizens from leaving and entering the country without giving specific reasons.

That statement alone contradicted the Malaysian Constitution, which states that every citizen has the right to freedom of movement. Because of that, I continued the legal battle by filing an appeal at the Court of Appeal, hoping for that "rare and limited edition" justice.

As I keep saying, this is not about justice for me. It is about justice for the country. So whether I win or lose, I would continue to use my cartoons to fight.

As a recipient for the Cartooning for Peace Award, I was offered the opportunity to display my cartoons opposite the United Nation's building at Lac Léman, Geneva.

I'm describing my cartoon to former Secretary General of the United Nations, Kofi Annan, who had officiated at the opening of my exhibition.

I received the Cartooning for Peace Award from Kofi Annan on May 3, 2016, in Geneva, Switzerland.

The United Nations congratulated me on my award.

Malaysian Communications and Multimedia Minister Salleh Said Keruak said my exhibition in Geneva was an effort to topple Prime Minister Najib. Screenshot of a news bulletin on TV3.

Deputy Prime Minister Zahid Hamidi, who was also the Home Minister, said he wanted the police to take action against me for my exhibition.

Following the exhibition in Geneva, I was banned from travelling indefinitely without my knowledge. I took this selfie at the Immigration counter at the Kuala Lumpur International Airport after I was informed of the ban by one of the personnel.

IGP Khalid Abu Bakar dared me to fight them. Screenshot from Malay Mail Online.

International organisations slammed the Malaysian government over my travel ban. They were Cartoonists Rights Network International, Cartooning for Peace Foundation, Cartoon Movement, Comic Book Legal Defence Fund, Committee to Protect Journalists, International Federation of Journalists, Wikipedia's Jimmy Wales Foundation. Screenshot of a news piece from Free Malaysia Today.

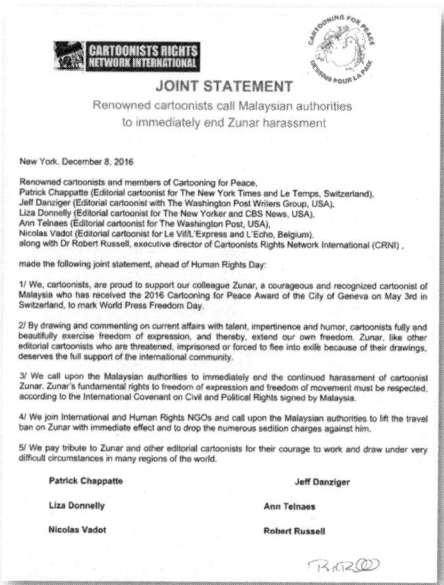

A joint statement from award-winning cartoonists from around the world condemning the travel ban and sedition charges against me. They were Patrick Chappatte, Liza Donnelly, Jeff Danzinger, Ann Teinaes, Nicolas Vadot and Robert Russell.

Prominent fugitive artist Ai Wei Wei was also among those who showed support.

United Nations (UN) Special Rapporteur Karima Bennoune urged the Malaysian government to remove my travel ban and drop my nine sedition charges.

Although I couldn't travel, one of my cartoons was displayed on a giant screen at the World Economic Forum in Davos on January 20, 2017.

Despite being unable to travel, I was still invited to deliver talks through Skype. Here I am giving a talk to an Amnesty International audience in Paris.

At the Kuala Lumpur High Court with my lawyer Eric Paulsen (left) and a group of supporters when I filed my travel ban challenge on December 7, 2016.

Pada 17.10.2016, ketika saya berada di Lapangan Terbang Antarabangsa Kuala Lumpur (KLIA) untuk menaiki pesawat ke Singapura, saya telah dihalang oleh pegawai imigresen dari melepasi pintu imigresen walaupun saya memiliki paspot yang sah (No. Paspot; A 34726525) dan tiket penerbangan yang sah.

Kini dikemukakan dan ditunjukkan kepada saya secara kolektif bertanda sebagai Ekshibit "ZAH-1" adalah sesalinan paspot saya dan tiket penerbangan saya yang mengandungi butir-butir di atas.

Saya dimaklumkan secara lisan oleh pegawai imigresen bahawa saya dihalang dari melepasi pintu imigresen atas arahan Ketua Polis Negara (KPN). Walaubagaimanapun pegawai tersebut tidak memberi apa-apa penjelasan lanjut.

A snippet of the court document on my travel ban challenge.

Me and my lawyers N. Surendran and Melissa Sasidaran during the travel ban challenge at the Malaysian High Court.

ME AGAINST GANGSTERS
Cartoon exhibition attacked and smashed

By not allowing me to travel, the government was trying to stop me from having exhibitions overseas.

The travel ban had also curtailed my overseas activities and campaigning for freedom of expression, which included several talks at universities. Previously, I had given talks at Cambridge, Oxford, the School of Oriental and African Studies (SOAS), University of California, Irvine (UC Irvine), and the University of Louisville, Kentucky.

However, I had to think positive and continue. So I began to plan my exhibition in Malaysia instead: I wanted it to be an open exhibition, similar to the one I had in Geneva, because an open exhibition meant that the cartoons would be shown to the public instead of being held in a museum or gallery where only art lovers would attend. I sent my proposal to the Selangor government and it was accepted.

I began holding "To Fight Through Cartoons" exhibitions — two weeks in Petaling Jaya, followed by another week in Shah Alam.

These exhibitions went smoothly without any disturbances. Then I planned to bring the exhibition to Penang. It would travel to several places in the state with the first being Komtar, then the Esplanade, followed by Bayan Baru. I had assigned two of my assistants, Azura and Megat Abdul Wahid, to facilitate this exhibition, including getting sponsorship from individuals.

The exhibition at Komtar was held on November 25, 2016, and was part of the George Town Literary Festival, which was held at the same time. It was a 20-panel billboard exhibition (4 x 6 feet), with each billboard having two drawings side by side. It was launched by Penang chief minister, Lim Guan Eng, and Penang state executive councilor, Abdul Malik Abul Kassim. During my speech, I explained that the travel ban was the reason why I wanted to hold the exhibition in Penang and why I chose an open concept: I wanted this exhibition to come to the people instead of people having to visit it at a designated place. At the exhibition, Azura and Megat set up a counter to sell my books to visitors. After the launch, people started buying the books and the sale went quite well. However, prior to that, in the morning, I saw many Umno members tweeting and condemning the exhibition. Some of the tweets went viral. But for me that was common, these individuals would do anything to condemn me.

Then we took a break for Friday prayers. At about 2.30pm, Azura, Megat and I returned to the exhibition. We were the only three there and were about to get ready to receive visitors. At around 3pm, a group of 50 to 60 people approached us, with a video camera. They were very aggressive. Their leader came up to me and introduced himself as the Penang Umno chief, Rafizal Abdul Rahim. He said he had come to ask me to take down the exhibits. I asked for the reason and he said the cartoons were humiliating to the prime minister and his wife. I said, "Well, this is my exhibition." He asked who had selected the works to be exhibited and I said I had done so myself. They asked me where were the cartoons about Opposition politician Lim Guan Eng and I explained that this was my exhibition, so I chose my own subject. "If you don't agree, you can do your own exhibition and choose your own subject," I told him.

My reply made them more aggressive because they didn't know how to respond. Then the group started to become rowdy. They started to push me, kick my exhibits, pull my shirt and kept pushing me further and demanded that I take down the cartoons. I didn't say anything. I just kept quiet because there was no point in reacting or retaliating against such individuals.

I think they were hoping for some physical reaction from me which could be used as news material on state-controlled television. Imagine if I had pushed them back, it would have been recorded and shown on prime-time news.

When I didn't react, they became even more aggressive. They pushed me harder, screamed and shouted loudly, and jumped around like monkeys. One of them pulled my collar from behind until I almost fell, but luckily, Megat managed to get a hold of me. Another one punched me on the face, but still I didn't react.

There was police presence, about five to six police officers at the scene, but they didn't do anything to stop them. One of the policemen, a Chinese man, put his arms around me to try and protect me. I think he did it on his own personal initiative. The other officers just continued looking without doing anything.

At the same time, this group also went after Azura who was at the counter. They shouted at her, calling her names. The chaos went on for half an hour and there was no sign of stopping.

The policeman pulled me and the gang leader, Rafizal, to one corner. He asked me to take down all of my artwork, which I declined to do at first, but I finally agreed as I didn't want to fight this group. I asked Megat to take down the exhibition. Some exhibits had already fallen down because the group had kicked the exhibition panels.

Despite taking down the artwork, the group still continued to harass me. They kicked, stepped and even and jumped on the fallen artwork. One person even spat in my face.

Throughout the entire episode, I was scared. Normally, when one faced any security issue, one would go to the police, but in this case even the police couldn't do anything. I was worried for my safety and I couldn't do anything about the thugs.

Luckily, someone arrived and stood beside me. His name was Wahab and he was a Silat master. He told me he had almost lost his cool. I told him not to do anything because they would turn the situation into a news broadcast about Zunar's supporters trying to beat people up. But the group became more aggressive and physical, and some of them even began throwing shoes at me and my artwork. Finally, the anti-riot police, the Federal Reserve Unit (FRU), arrived at the scene.

Only when the FRU arrived did the group begin to disperse. Before that, they didn't care about the police because the police didn't take action against them. The incident went on for about one hour. After that, a few journalists arrived and I made an announcement to them that I had to cancel this exhibition along with my other planned exhibitions at Bayan Baru and the Esplanade due to security reasons.

As the artwork were big pieces, I needed a place to store them temporarily. I called Dr Hew Kuan Yau from Penang's Asia Comic Cultural Museum and asked if I could store them at the museum because his place was just next to the exhibition venue. He agreed, so I moved all of the artwork to the museum's store.

Later on, Azura and Megat went back to their hotel. I needed to attend the launch of the George Town Literary Festival at the Black Kettle at 6pm. Fearing for my security, I called my friend, Zulkifli Mohamad, who worked in Komtar, to drive me to the Black Kettle.

At the launch, Lim Guan Eng mentioned in his speech the incident in Komtar, and he said this was not Penang's way. After the event, I spent the night at my friend Lee Khai's condominium, but I didn't tell my assistants where I stayed. At around 10pm, I received a call from Azura, asking where I was. I told her I was staying at a friend's house. She said the police were looking for me. They had called her and asked, "Where is Zunar?" She had replied that she didn't know and then she asked what was the matter. The police replied that they just wanted to make sure I was safe.

I was quite sceptical about this and told Azura not to tell the police about my location. The next morning, I read a news report that Rafizal and the Umno youths had lodged a police report against me over the incident.

I couldn't understand what their plans were. The reporters had called me, asking if I would be making a police report against them. I said I won't because I didn't want to engage with barbaric persons. I simply didn't want to deal with them. There's a Malay saying, "Biarkan si luncai terjun dengan labu-labunya." (To let others do what they want. I don't care.)

The next day, I continued to stay at the condominium. At around 3pm, I received a call from a police officer who asked me to come to the police headquarters in Jalan Pattani, not far from Komtar. I asked about the purpose and he said this was due to the incident at Komtar and they wanted me to assist in the investigation. I said I couldn't make it for 3pm as I had just gotten back from meeting a friend and I asked if I could go at 5pm. He agreed. I was not sure about the situation and decided to be cautious and get a lawyer to accompany me. After making a few calls, I managed to get a lawyer, RSN Rayer.

We arrived at the police station at around 5.30pm and were welcomed by two police officers. They asked me to take a seat and wait for a while for their colleague who would be speaking to me. After a while, a police officer came and told me that they were conducting an investigation under Section 504 of the Penal Code and the Sedition Act. For that, he said he would have to arrest me.

I was shocked. How could this be to assist him with the investigation? I didn't understand because I was not the one who made the ruckus at Komtar. I told him that he should arrest Umno Youth instead. He said he was following instructions. I asked, "Whose instructions?" He replied, "I can't tell you. But we're going to arrest you and confiscate your artwork that was exhibited at Komtar."

He asked where the artwork was kept and I told him they were at Penang's Asia Comic Cultural Museum, located next to the Komtar building. I told him as it was already 6.30pm, I was not sure if the place was open. I asked him if I could call Dr Hew and he said to go ahead.

I called Dr Hew and told him the police would be coming to the museum to confiscate all my artwork. He said he was already at home but would return to the museum. I told the police that they could go over. But I also told the police that I had forgotten to inform Dr Hew when they would be arriving at the museum, and asked if I could text him about the police's arrival time. The police allowed me to do so. But this was actually a tactic to text Dr Hew to inform all of Penang's reporters to go to the museum immediately.

I then heard the officer give instructions to his men to get the car to go to Komtar. I could have just let them go by car, but I told him the pieces of artwork were too big to be transported by car. I suggested that they obtain a lorry or truck to transport the artwork. After some time, they managed to get a truck and they brought me to the museum in a separate car.

When we arrived, there were many reporters waiting for us. It was a good tactic. I was in handcuffs moving from the police car to the lift to go up to the second floor where the artwork was kept. The reporters followed us to the second floor. Some of them took pictures and videos. The police scolded them and told them not to take pictures. Together with Dr Hew, I brought the police to the museum's store where the artwork was kept. The police started taking the pieces of artwork away by trolley, using the elevator to load them into the truck one by one.

The police then brought me back to the station, where I had to sign the "Borang Bongkar" (Confiscation Form). Before I signed it, I made sure that they counted the pieces of the artwork one by one. I asked Rayer to take a photo of each piece of artwork. They then handed me over to the Investigating Officer, (IO) ASP Khalil. He then sent me to the lock-up downstairs.

I was brought to the lock-up in handcuffs, where there were several officers waiting. ASP Khalil asked me to go to a separate room to change: I had to remove my clothes and change into the lock-up attire of purple shorts and shirt. I had to spend a night in the police lock-up.

The next day, after breakfast, the police brought me to the George Town Magistrate Court to obtain a remand order. I arrived again in handcuffs and there were a few supporters at the venue. I heard one lady shouting, "Hidup Zunar!" (Long live Zunar!). I smiled at her and said, "Thank you."

In the courtroom, there were five lawyers waiting to represent me: Rayer, Ramkarpal Singh, Cheah Kah Peng, Lee Khai and Mathan. I told them this had to be a new record with five lawyers for a remand order proceeding!

During the proceedings, the police asked for another four days of remand to keep me in the lock-up because, according to them, they wanted to investigate me further. My lawyers argued about the necessity when all the evidence was already in their possession. My lawyers added that Zunar's artwork had already been taken and what the police needed was just one statement from me, which would take no more than one to two hours.

The magistrate finally agreed to give a one-day remand order. This meant that the police would have to release me by 7pm at the latest that same day. I was then brought back to the police station and the police officer put me in the office instead of the lock-up to take my statement. I told ASP Khalil, the officer who was to take my statement that I would use my right not to answer any question.

Among the questions asked was this: "Do you realise that many people are unhappy with your exhibition? This is the reason why many had gone to Komtar to protest." Off the record, I told the officer that with a 30-million population in Malaysia, only 60 people had protested against my exhibition. So how could he justify that statement?

Another comment put forward to me was that my exhibition had created disharmony. That was the reason the police had to arrest me. At this point, I understood the game. The incident in Komtar was actually a reverse process to stop me. The main purpose was to arrest me. But I did nothing wrong in that exhibition. So they had to create chaos to justify my arrest. This was why the incident was followed with a police report by Umno Youth.

After the interrogation ended, I was sent downstairs to another room to have my photograph and fingerprints taken. I was surprised when one of the police officers asked for permission to take a selfie with me. At 6pm, I was released and went outside with Rayer to give a statement to the journalists who were waiting outside the police station.

The George Town Literary Festival was still on and the organiser had arranged for a quick event at the Black Kettle for me to launch my book, *Wasabi*. I was told there were many people there, but there was also a heavy police presence. Rayer advised me not to go because he had been informed by the police that if I went, they would arrest me again. I decided not to go because it was pointless to go there to get arrested yet again.

The police continued with their investigations. Penang state councilor, Abdul Malik Abdul Kassim, who had allowed me to hold the exhibition was investigated under the Sedition Act. Separately, my friend Lee Khai was also investigated for allowing me to stay in his condominium.

I had planned to hold another exhibition in Penang, titled "Ketawa Pink Pink", a few months later, on July 29, 2017. I wanted to do it openly at Beach Street, where the road was closed every Saturday for a street festival. I discussed with the organiser, Ving, about getting permission for the exhibition and she agreed, and said it would be arranged.

I then made a poster about the upcoming exhibition and announced on social media that I would go to Penang again. Suddenly, I saw a poster by Umno Youth being circulated on social media, calling their "friends" to "visit" my exhibition. This was the same group that had disrupted my exhibition at Komtar.

The word "visit" used in the Umno Youth poster could be interpreted as another round of chaos that would be created by them. Seeing this poster, I was unsure about continuing with the exhibition. One night prior to the exhibition, I received a call from the Penang police saying that they would arrest me if I continued with the exhibition.

Based on my experience at Komtar, I knew what their tactic would be. To me, it was all clearly scripted. I felt it would be better to spoil their script than turn up to get myself arrested. For me, I didn't want to be arrested unnecessarily. I would do something that was within my rights, but if I could see that I would be arrested for it, then I would not. The authorities were employing tactics of gangsterism and the police against me this time in order to stop my exhibition.

A month later, I initiated legal action against the Penang police. It was difficult to get a lawyer from Penang to file a suit against the police. After months of searching, I finally got a senior lawyer, Cecil Rajendra, who was ready to take my case pro bono. I went to Penang several times to meet him to discuss the case.

On March 26, 2018, through Cecil, I sent a Notice of Demand to the police to reply within 14 days. In the notice, I asked the police to return my confiscated pieces of artwork and to apologise for my unlawful arrest. But they didn't reply. In July, Cecil sent another letter to the police, but they still did not reply.

On November 12, 2018, Cecil filed a legal suit on my behalf at the Penang High Court on my illegal arrest and the confiscation of my artwork. I named Northeast District senior criminal investigating officer ASP Rusli Tipu, the Inspector General of Police and the Malaysian government as defendants. I demanded that the police return all 20 pieces of my artwork and pay compensation.

As I was not allowed to hold exhibitions overseas due to my travel ban,
I started to hold exhibitions locally in Malaysia.
This is my exhibition in Komtar shopping complex, Penang.

In fighting against me, the government started a new tactic of using violence. A few hours after the launch, about 60 Umno Youth members stormed into my exhibition and started to push and pull me. They forced me to remove my artworks.

When I declined, the mob became even more rude and aggressive. They shouted and screamed at me.

For more than one hour, they surrounded me and continuously harassed me verbally and physically.

The situation was so tense that even the police was unable to control them.

The group then continued destroying my artwork by kicking and jumping on them.

The anti-riot police (Federal Reserve Unit – FRU) had to be called in when the situation went too far out of control with the possibility of turning violent. I had to cancel my exhibition.

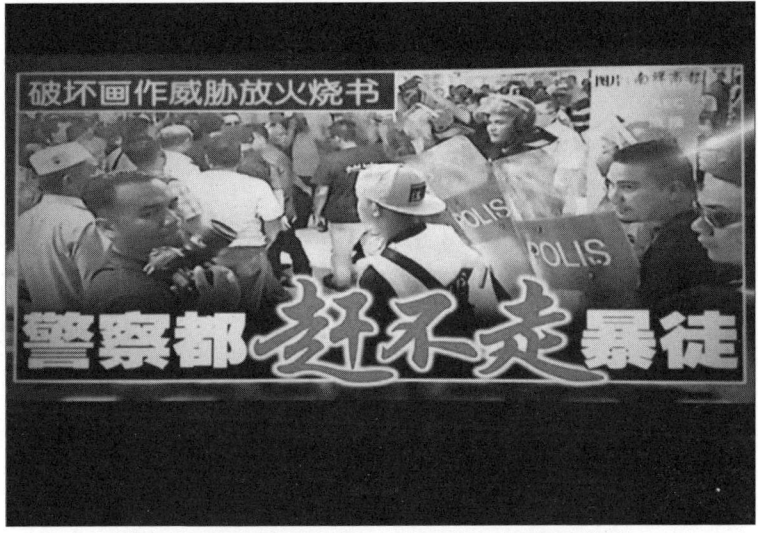

"Even the police is unable to stop them." A headline from a Chinese language newspaper the next day.

Another report on the incident by *The Star*.

The police then confiscated all 40 pieces of my exhibited artwork.

The police took away all the artwork using a truck.

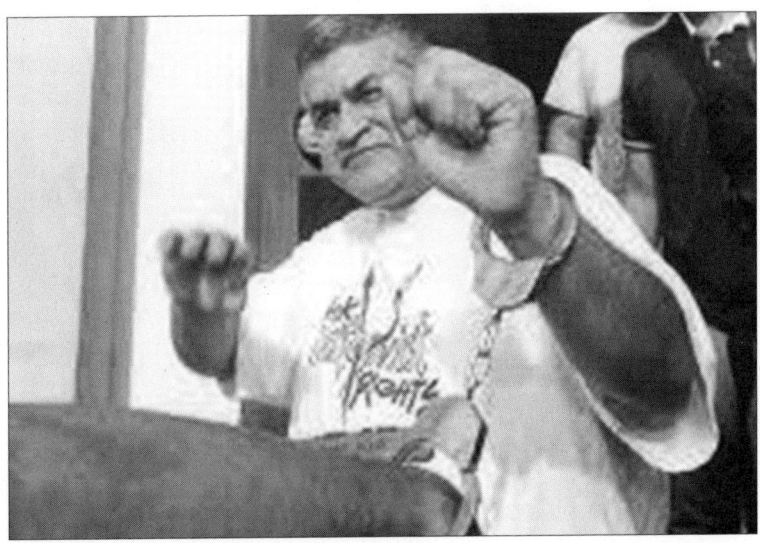

Instead of arresting the Umno Youth members, the police arrested me under the Sedition Act.

My arrest in Penang was reported by international website, Mashable.

THE ILLEGAL TEA
Detrimental to parliamentary democracy

A WEEK AFTER THE KOMTAR INCIDENT, I held a meeting with five members of the Independent Cartoonist Group (Kumpulan Kartunis Independen, KKI). KKI is a group of independent cartoonists formed in 2009. It is a loosely structured group which shares artwork and experiences, and also undertakes exhibitions and programmes once in a while.

The meeting was attended by Cherise Boey, Johnny Ong, Lawrence Jebaraj, Megat and myself. I told them that I had to recover my losses which were estimated to be between RM50,000 to RM60,000 (US$15,000) after Umno Youth had disrupted the exhibition and destroyed my artwork at Komtar.

How would we recover such a huge loss? After half an hour, we came up with the idea to hold a fund-raising event. It was to be called "Tea with Zunar" and it would be held at the KL Selangor Chinese Assembly on December 17, 2016. The entrance ticket would be RM50 and participants would be served curry puffs, fried noodles and tea. There would also be a small exhibition and a talk by me, together with a question and answer session.

However, even if 100 people attended, I would only get RM5,000 (US$1,200) and this would still not be enough to cover the loss. So we planned to sell a set of my cartoon books. This set would have all the rare books that were very hard to find. It was a premium set of books that could not be bought from bookshops or even online.

This set consisted of 10 titles and was priced at RM500 each. The collection, together with some donations, would have been enough to cover half of the amount needed. On top of that, we also planned to sell t-shirts and mugs. I asked Lawrence to help with the hall booking and to arrange the facilities, while Cherise, Johnny and Megat would help me with the exhibition and sell tickets. The other KKI members, Jonos and Yong, helped to prepare 100 sets of the books. The plan was to have supporters come in at 4pm, have some tea and snacks, then proceed to a room where I would talk about what had happened at Komtar.

So we packed around 100 sets which consisted of 1,000 of these books and 300 of loose copies. On the day of the event, Jonos and Yong arrived earlier to help set up.

I arrived later with Megat and Lawrence at 3pm. The event hall was on the first floor. Downstairs, I saw about 20 people loitering at the entrance, and some of them were making phone calls. Even though they looked familiar, it didn't cross my mind that they were Special Branch police officers. It didn't occur to me that there would be any arrest as it was just a tea party.

It was raining that day, so we started a little later than 4pm. When the rain stopped, people began arriving and they started to have tea at the foyer. Lawrence and Megat had set up a booth and the two of them were handling book sales while Cherise and Johnny entertained the guests. I was inside a room preparing my speech without concern for what was happening outside.

A few minutes later, I saw a uniformed police officer with two plainclothes personnel enter the room. The one in uniform introduced himself as DSP M Gunalan from Dang Wangi Police Station, while the other two were the ones I had seen downstairs. Gunalan then said he was going to arrest me and I had to follow him to the police station. I asked him under what offence and under which law. He said he could not tell.

Normally when the police want to make an arrest, they will inform the person to be arrested about the offence and the law under which they will be arrested. But this officer said he would only tell me at the police station.

Prior to that, without my knowledge, the police had already arrested Lawrence and Megat outside. They also confiscated all the books and t-shirts, but I didn't know because I was in the room.

The police handcuffed me and brought me downstairs. I was about to be brought to the police car when I could hear commotion upstairs but I could not see what was happening. I could hear loud yelling and people protesting. They stopped bringing me to the car and made me wait downstairs with another officer. I later found out that they had arrested two of my fans, Jimmy Wong Chee Wai and Toong Ah Tee.

They were arrested because they had asked DSP Gunalan why he had arrested me. Instead of explaining to them, Gunalan had reacted by scolding and handcuffing them. He then shouted to everyone at the scene, especially those who took pictures and videos, including Azura and another supporter, Ginie Lim.

Ginie came downstairs to speak with me. One of the police officers followed her and demanded that she delete all pictures and videos which were taken. I asked her, "Have you uploaded the materials onto social media?" She said yes and I told her, "Okay, delete in front of the police officer."

After half an hour, I saw the police bringing Megat, Lawrence, Jimmy and Toong downstairs. The police then confiscated all 1,300 of my books and around 100 t-shirts and mugs which were supposed to be sold at the event. At the entrance of the building, there were two police cars waiting. Also present were hundreds of supporters. Among them was a lawyer and former Bersih chairman, Ambiga Sreenevasan, who tried to ask the police which offence I was being arrested for. But Gunalan couldn't and didn't want to say anything.

At the same time, I also asked my supporters if any of them were lawyers. One person, Nicole Tan, raised her hand. I asked her if she could assist the five of us at the police station, to which she agreed. We were taken to Dang Wangi Police Station in one car and Nicole followed us in DSP Gunalan's car.

After arriving at the police station, we were brought to the eighth floor. The police did not put us in the lock-up yet because according to them, they were waiting for instructions from Bukit Aman.

Lembah Pantai Member of Parliament, Nurul Izzah, and Batu Member of Parliament, Tian Chua, arrived to visit us. Around 10pm, DSP Gunalan came to me and said that I was arrested under section 124C of the Penal Code for activity detrimental to parliamentary democracy.

This was the same law they had used against then Bersih chairman, Maria Chin Abdullah. Under this law, the police is given wide powers to arrest people without trial for two weeks. This made me really scared.

After waiting for a few hours, DSP Gunalan said we won't be detained in the lock-up but will be released soon after we had given our statements. Megat, Lawrence, Jimmy, Toong and I had to give our statements separately. For Toong and Jimmy, they were charged under a different law for obstructing the police in carrying out their duties.

It took two hours for all of us to give our statements. All the statements were taken in the presence of our lawyer, Nicole. We were all advised by Nicole to use our right not to answer any questions except personal particulars.

While giving my statement, the police officer informed me that I was doing an illegal activity in selling banned books. I told him that couldn't be right as the ban on the books had been lifted by the court. He said three of the books, *Pirates of the Carry-BN*, *The Conspiracy to Imprison Anwar* and *Komplot Penjarakan Anwar* were banned in 2014. I told the police officer that I didn't know about this. Usually, the government would make a public statement or inform the author about such a ban.

The officer then showed me a form which revealed that the ban on the books had been gazetted in 2014. I said I did not know about this because I was not informed. In my mind, I didn't do anything wrong because I didn't know these books were banned. We were released at about 1am.

On August 16, 2017, I filed a legal suit against the police to challenge my arrest and demanded that my books and merchandise be returned. I was represented by Latheefa Koya and N Surendran from Lawyers for Liberty.

During the case management stage, before the trial started, the court suggested that a mediation be held. Mediation is a process whereby two parties attempt to settle a case outside the court. In this case, mediation would be between myself and DSP Gunalan on behalf of the police. The mediation was set for December 15, 2017, in a special room at the Kuala Lumpur High Court Complex in Jalan Duta. I went with Latheefa and Gunalan was accompanied by his Deputy Public Prosecutor from the Attorney-General's office. The mediation session was held before a Court Registrar. Even though a lawyer and a Deputy Public Prosecutor were present, only myself and DSP Gunalan were allowed to speak.

Throughout the session, the police offered to settle the case and return my books. I told them it was not about the returning of books. The question was about my unlawful arrest and the confiscation of my books. So I told Gunalan that he had to be responsible for this.

At the end, I told the Registrar that I would only settle this matter outside the court under two conditions:

1. The police had to issue a public apology in the newspapers over my unlawful arrest.

2. The police also had to pay me for the damages I had suffered because of the arrest and confiscation of the books.

Gunalan declined the two conditions and the mediation ended without any decision. This meant that the matter would be referred back to the court for trial.

A week later, on January 5, 2018, Jimmy and Toong were charged separately at the Magistrate's Court in Kuala Lumpur for obstructing a public officer during the "Tea With Zunar" event. Both of them were charged after the mediation had failed. For me, it was not a coincidence, it could well have been a tactic to punish me.

On September 10, 2015, I had released my cartoon book, *Sapuman, Man of Steal*. In this book, I had depicted the prime minister of Malaysia, Najib Razak, as a superhero, Sapuman. Sapu in Malay means "steal". It was a parody of the film, *Superman, Man of Steel*.

The cartoon showed the prime minister flying in a superhero costume and holding a bag of money which amounted to RM2.6 billion (US$681 million). It was widely reported that he had received this amount of money in his private bank account as part of the 1Malaysia Development Berhad (1MDB) scandal.

On October 3, 2017, two years after publication, the government banned *Sapuman*. The ban came a month after Najib visited the United States president, Donald Trump. During the visit, Najib had promised to give Trump billions of dollars to "save" the American economy. This was very funny and comical, and I came up with a cartoon depicting Najib as Sapuman flying to the US with money to help Trump.

I suspected it was because of this cartoon that the government banned *Sapuman*. On January 2, 2018, I filed a suit at the High Court in Kuala Lumpur to challenge the ban.

During this time, I was also investigated for another cartoon, which depicted Najib using five public funds to pay the 1MDB debt. I was called up, on November 29, 2017, to give a statement to the police under Section 233 of the Communications and Multimedia Act.

"Sapuman, Man of Steal" became a bit of a popular slogan. The *New York Times* contacted me for permission to use my cartoon for one of their headlines in reference to the corruption scandal in Malaysia, which I granted.

After the incident in Penang, I began planning a fundraising event to recover the RM60,000 I had lost.

The poster for the fundraising event.

The event was open to my fans and friends.

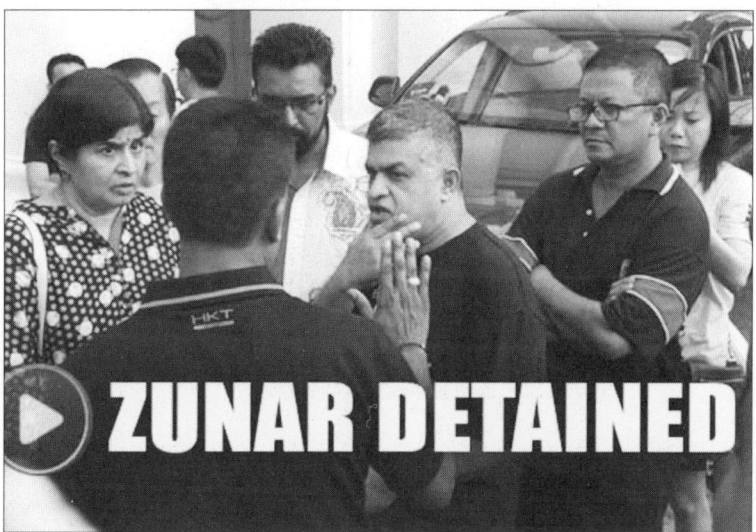

Before the event started, I was arrested by the police under Section 124C of the Penal Code for activities that were purportedly detrimental to parliamentary democracy. Many activists have been detained without trial under this law.

Despite my fear, I still managed to smile at my supporters
before being taken away in a police car.

Meanwhile, 1,000 of my books and merchandise were confiscated and taken away to Dang Wangi Police Station.

Me and my supporters, upon our release after being detained and interrogated for nine hours. Together with us is our lawyer, Nicole Tan.

I filed a legal suit against the police to challenge my arrest and demand that my books and merchandise be returned.

The government continued to harass me.
My latest book, *Sapuman Man of Steal*, was banned on October 3, 2017.

Then I was investigated under the Communications and
Multimedia Act for drawing this cartoon.

CHAPTER 15
STRUGGLE IS AN ENDLESS MARATHON

STRUGGLE IS AN ENDLESS MARATHON
If you cannot beat them, laugh at them

At this juncture, I was facing a dilemma and real fear.

First of all, I was on a travel ban and could not travel abroad. So I held events in Malaysia, but I was faced with arrest, hooliganism, and also prosecution. In simple terms, I could not go out but I could only go in — in to prison!

I needed to think long and hard about this. I met a few friends to seek their opinion about my situation and many of them sincerely advised me to get out of the country because if I went to prison, I would not be able to draw cartoons anymore. This would defeat my original purpose of using cartoons to save my country. But if I lived outside Malaysia, I could still draw, even though it would not be impactful enough. I could still do something to push for reform, and so I agreed to this.

A friend devised a plan for me to escape to another country. He already had a route in mind. The plan was like this: I needed to go to a particular place on the Thailand border and there waiting for me would be a pre-arranged taxi; the driver would bring me across the border without having to deal with immigration. Everything would be taken care of. He told me not to worry, the taxi driver would help me.

As I crossed the border, another person would wait for me with a car and he would bring me to a hotel. And then I would be a free man. The plan would continue into the next morning, when I would need to take a train or bus to Bangkok. Then board a plane to either London or the United States, Switzerland, Norway, Sweden, etc, and apply for asylum. This friend would also provide me with the air ticket and expenses for the first few months. The plan was already in place and it was up to me.

I also contacted a friend who had experience working with an organisation that rescues artists who have problems with their governments. The Norway-based organization is called the International Cities of Refuge Network (ICORN). Their focus is on rescuing artists, writers and journalists in trouble. This friend put me in contact with the person in charge of such matters. They then asked me to open a new email account because they did not trust my public email as it could be hacked by the government. They sent me a form to register to be rescued.

I completed the form and returned it to them. Then I had to make a decision. This was to be done as secretively as possible to avoid leaks. I did not tell my wife and family. The more people who knew, the less chance for me to succeed.

I thought deeply about this for a very long time. There were many words that came to my mind. Yes, I had fear, but responsibility is bigger than fear.

At the same time, if I stayed and went to prison, I would not be able to keep fighting. This was a conflict between my mind and my heart. This was a big dilemma and I kept thinking and thinking about it day and night. Finally, I had a revelation: if I went out, I could only save myself, but if I stayed, I could save the country. So I chose to save my country and complete my mission. Even though I had to make a sacrifice, if this was for the benefit of the people, then I had to do it. I was more motivated than ever.

I then went back to my studio and looked back at all my cartoons and did a long introspection on how to improve and make my work more impactful.

At the same time, the mood in the country was not so good. Many have said to me that they have been fighting for so long. They have given up and did not want to care anymore. Some have even said they wanted to migrate.

However, I told them, "Please don't give up. We cannot simply stop and not do anything. We have to continue to push for change."

A struggle is an endless marathon. The winners are those who keep themselves on track and moving forward. It does not matter how we move, by walking, running or even crawling; as long as we keep moving, we will reach our destination one day.

Even if we do not see the change in our lifetime, it will be a precious gift for the future generations.

The 14th General Elections was set to be held in three months' time, on May 9, 2018. I had to work harder and produce more cartoons in order to create awareness among Malaysians, and use the opportunity to push for change.

I needed to double up my efforts and I decided to venture into another medium: I wanted to animate my cartoons to make them more impactful on social media and on the younger members of the Malaysian community.

I didn't know how to do animation nor did I know any animators. I posted an advertisement on my Facebook page that I urgently needed animators to help me with an election campaign and those who were interested should write to me. Some wrote in and named their price, but I couldn't hire them because I didn't have money. I almost cancelled the project as there were no animators able to help in my situation.

However, a month before voting day, I was at Midvalley shopping complex when I was approached by a fan. He said he liked my cartoons. We began talking and he asked if I would like to have coffee with him. I agreed and during our chat, he said if I wanted to animate my cartoons, he would be able to help.

I told him that I was looking for an animator, but I could not afford to pay for one. He said payment was not an issue. He was an experienced animator and wanted to animate my cartoons because he had the same mission to change the government. He was godsent to me.

However, he said he would only help if he didn't have to use his real name because he was afraid of retaliation by the government. His real name is Sine Ng. I changed it to "Anis" in the videos.

Most of the cartoons he worked on were one-piece cartoons which he animated by adding movement and sound. He created the animations very fast because it took him only a day to work on each piece of cartoon. The results were short, lively animations which were less than a minute in duration, which I uploaded on Facebook, Twitter, Instagram and YouTube. After they were released, we received good responses from viewers.

As the election mood became hot, I discovered that there were so many people who had registered as new voters. Some of them were old and illiterate. For them, I drew a cartoon as a step-by-step guide on how to cast a vote. I also drew cartoons to remind people that we were the ones who were paying for all the corruption in the country and if we didn't vote for change now, we would only have ourselves to blame.

It was now or never. I had to come out with very funny yet strong cartoons with an inspiring message that would make a difference. The best way was to make them laugh at the government. So I needed to provide material for the people to laugh at the governing regime. This was one of the effective ways to kick them out. For this purpose, I released my best ever book called *Ketawa Pink Pink* during the election campaign.

The cartoons in this book were more dynamic than ever. They highlighted the very serious subject of corruption, especially the 1MDB scandal. But it was drawn in a lighthearted, funny and colourful way in order to get the people to feel comfortable reading it. When they read it, I wanted them to understand that the corruption affected their lives. Unless they pushed for change, they would be suffering for the rest of their lives.

The cartoons were dominated by the colour pink. This was to get female voters to connect to the book. Females form the majority of voters in this country. If they read my cartoons and understood the issue and my message, then change would be possible.

There were many cartoons in the book which compared the lifestyle of the prime minister's wife, Rosmah, with that of a normal housewife. I hoped that the female voters would become emotional and responsive when they see the prime minister's wife with a Birkin bag, a diamond ring and all the expensive accessories. Sometimes in the cartoons, I compared what the housewives had and what Rosmah had. For instance, Rosmah had Prada while they only ate *pratha* (bread).

I hoped that they would get angry when they see this, while having to pay so much in taxes. Through the cartoons, they would understand that they were actually the ones paying for the corruption. I hoped that they would then translate this realisation into votes. If the majority of female and male voters shifted their support, a change was possible. This was the objective of my cartoons.

I knew the people were angry; we were all angry because corruption was slowly eating away at our country, but I wanted to push for change in a positive way — turn your anger into laughter!

I conveyed the message that everybody needed to do their part through my cartoons. If you were a writer, you could write for change; if you were a singer, you could sing for change; if you were a painter, you could paint for change. Even if you have a dog and the dog could bite the corruptor's leg, it would also be considered a big contribution. For those who did not know what to do, the big contribution they could make was to share my cartoons, which were free of charge and without copyright.

Following this, people started to share and forward my cartoons to their friends, family, colleagues and neighbours, as well as Malaysians overseas through WhatsApp.

I saw that the feedback was very positive. Many people thanked me for my cartoons because they could now see clearly the corruption in Malaysia and how it affected everyone. They said they would vote for change this time. People of all ages, professions, social classes and races gave feedback to me that my cartoons had led to a change in their minds. A 60-year-old lady told me that she had voted for the government her entire life, but this time she would vote for the Opposition. According to her, what had made her change her mind was my book, *Ketawa Pink Pink*.

My message is to laugh and keep laughing at them. No regime in the world can stand if you laugh at them. Laughter is the best protest. If you cannot beat them, laugh at them. Laugh, laugh, laugh until they fall.

On May 9, 2018, the people of Malaysia casted their vote. The Barisan Nasional regime was defeated and the new coalition Pakatan Harapan came into power.

My mission to fight through cartoons was accomplished.

In order to help people understand how corruption affected their lives, I used the character of the wife of the prime minister as a symbol.

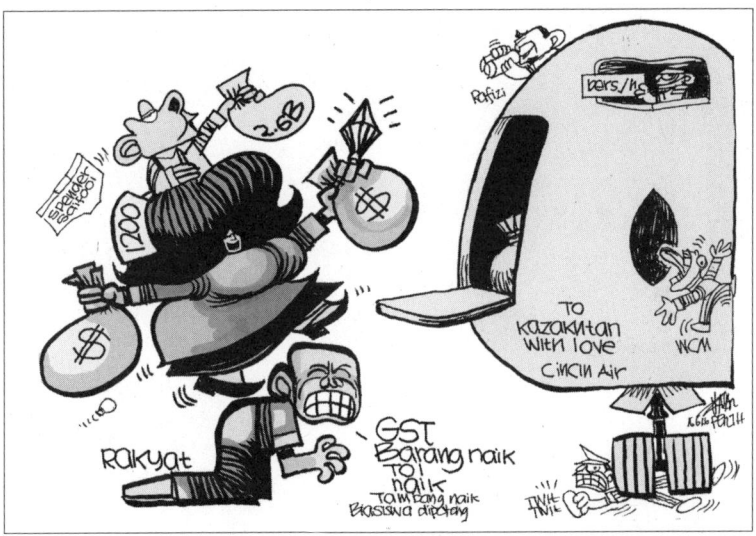

I presented my latest book to Justice Mohamad Ariff Md Yusof when he retired, not because he lifted the ban on my books, but because he was brave enough to uphold the law when he instructed the government to do so.

A few weeks before the 14th general elections, I doubled up my efforts by creating animated cartoons to make them more impactful on social media. I collaborated with experienced animator Sine Ng.

After I introduced a new way of cartooning, people of all ages, professions, social classes and races began to show their support for me and engage with my cartoons.

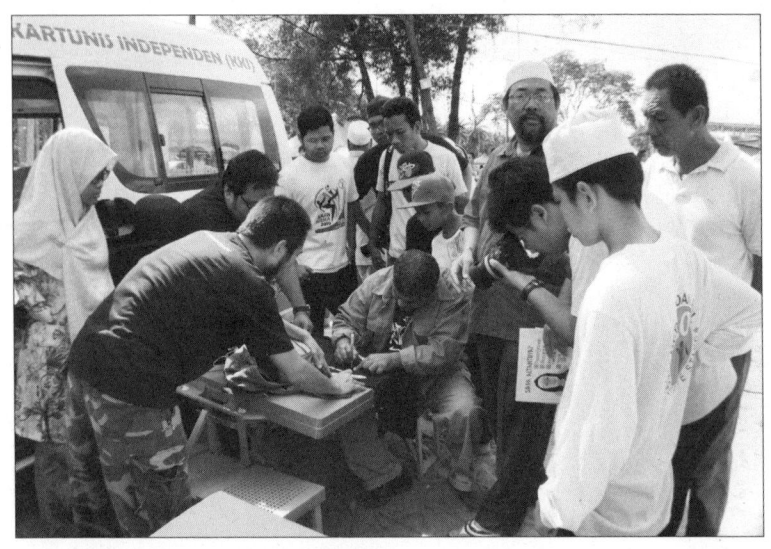

On the ground, I also gave talks to Malaysians on why they needed to make a change.

Fans thought of ingenious ways to avoid getting into trouble with the law in their attempts to show their support for me.

Online, Malaysians were positive and thanked me
for showing how corruption affected Malaysia.

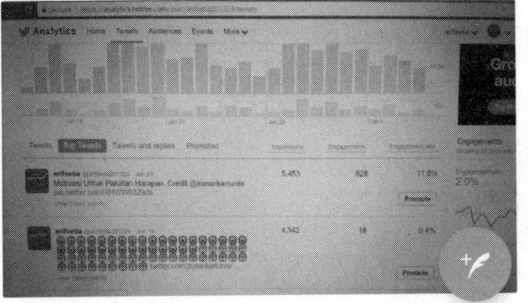

Kahuna Nui ✓ @Duurianne · 5m
I grew up with Lat's Kampung Boy & his teacher's funny hairdo.

My children grow up with @zunarkartunis

The ring & bikmama's funny hairdo.

what............????¿¿¿¿¿iiiiiiiii$$$$$$$$$$$$$$$$$$$$$$$$$$$$$$$
Like · Reply · 1 hr

Sop Tawau Ade ade jer!
Like · Reply · 1 hr

Stanley Sim 😁 funny! but true!
Like · Reply · 45 mins

Sharon Sidhu Zunar, you are very creative and talented. Reading your drawings always makes me laugh till my eye makeup runs ✌️✌️✌️✌️✌️ ✌️
Like · Reply · 35 mins

Red's Streetfighter Mmg lawak pagi lah
Like · Reply · 3 hrs

Terry Teh LOL...
Like · Reply · 3 hrs

Chew Chee Kien Nice one

James Yap The pen is always mightier than the sword...... keep the course, fight the cause..... God or Gods (whatever the reader's choice may be) willing, the truth will be made known to Malaysia's future generations. ✌️
Like · Reply · Message · 8 · March 22 at 6:03pm

Mary VSheila Absolutely respect you Zunar, a real man with principles, moral standards and a spine! Topped up with an amazing creativity n talent that makes me laugh, angry, upset and aware all at the same time scrutinizing every masterpiece you publish. My prayer is for God to bless and protect you always. THANK YOU.
Like · Reply · Message · 2 · March 23 at 4:01am

Theresa Bangah You are indeed one of many malaysian patriots....and a very responsible cartoonist without fear or favours....carry on your good works which is also recognised internationally...
Like · Reply · Message · March 23 at 12:27pm

Lay Leng Tan Anyone that brings shame to a country is the biggest jokers, therefore, Zunar makes the best choice. If I have the talent like Zunar, definitely I will also choose this 2 clowns.
Like · Reply · Message · 2 · March 22 at 7:08pm

Struggle is an Endless Marathon 245

 Mohammad Azmi Abdul Rahim Everyone will buy your books of cartoons if the authorities are democratic and support free expression !!
Like · Reply · Message · 1 · March 22 at 8:26pm

 Alex Lim My highest salute to you Zunar. You are not only very talented but have high principal and moral but bravery to go with it
Like · Reply · Message · 1 · March 23 at 8:23pm

 Ned Ghani Cartoonist have rights too...after all they are humans not cartoons.! They draw cartoons...
Like · Reply · Message · 1 · March 22 at 9:07pm

 Pitfong Jong Salute! To your talent and principles! I like your work, a lot!♥
Like · Reply · Message · 1 · March 22 at 9:09pm

 Seng Wee Zunar TQ for representing me as a Malaysians in your work Your earn my respect and salute 👍
Like · Reply · Message · 2 · March 23 at 10:16am

 Shiva Kumaar Arumugam This is self expression and responsibilities.I would do the same if I were you.
Like · Reply · Message · 1 · March 23 at 1:45pm

 Citizen Nades R Well said. We have a sacred duty to our fellow citizens.
Like · Reply · Message · 2 · March 23 at 5:44am
↳ 1 Reply

 Ibnu Saad How do you move carrying balls that big?
Like · Reply · Message · 2 · March 22 at 9:23pm

 Christopher Lee shared Zunar Cartoonist Fan Club's post.
March 23 at 9:22am ·

Well done Zunar! God bless you! So very well said. We don't have enough people like you, Zunar!
Show Attachment

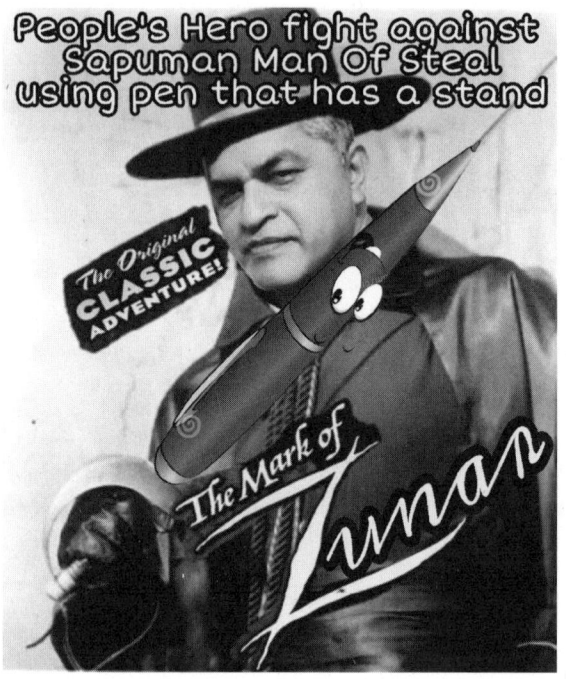

I drew this cartoon on May 10, 2018, to celebrate the people's victory in the general elections.

The New York Times used my cartoon's title "Man of Steal" to report on the fall of Najib Razak.

EPILOGUE

May 14, 2018 — The travel ban on Zunar is lifted.

July 31, 2018 — All nine sedition charges against Zunar are dropped.

August 9, 2018 — The ban on *Sapuman Man of Steal* is lifted.

October 18, 2018 — The police return 1,000 of Zunar's cartoon books and 100 t-shirts along with mugs seized during the Tea With Zunar event.

November 12, 2018 — Zunar files a civil suit to get the Penang police to return his confiscated artwork. The case is still ongoing.

December 13, 2018 — The police return Zunar's confiscated phone after four years.

April 4, 2019 — The court orders the government to pay damages to Zunar for banning *Sapuman Man of Steal*.

I still continue to draw about the new government.

Thank you to Malaysiakini, *The Star*, *The New Straits Times*, *Berita Harian*, Free Malaysia Today, Cilisos, AFP, AP, Reuters, BBC, Al Jazeera, mediarakyat, Aliran, Din Merican, Melissa Goh, *The Sun Daily*, *Sinar Harian*, *Kosmo*, *Harian Metro*, *Utusan*, *Bernama*, *The Wall Street Journal*, *The Independent*, Khairul Ryezal, Manan Vatsyayana, Yahoo News Singapore, Wikipedia, Getty Images, Counter Currents.org, Zunar.my and many others for the images in this book.

ABOUT THE AUTHOR

Photo by Yong Norliza Kassim

ZUNAR IS A POLITICAL CARTOONIST from Malaysia, who has been drawing editorial cartoons for over 30 years. With his slogan, "How Can I be Neutral, Even My Pen Has a Stand", he exposes corruption and abuse of power committed by the government of Malaysia through his art.

Zunar has been arrested and detained for drawing cartoons that challenged official views. His books have been banned by the Malaysian government and his office raided by law enforcement officers. The factories that printed his books have also been raided and vendors throughout the country were often warned not to sell his books.

In 2015, Zunar was selected by Amnesty International as the first Malaysian for their biggest annual international campaign, 'Write for Rights (#W4R) 2015'. His various international awards received over the years include the Cartooning For Peace Award 2016 (Geneva) and the International Press Freedom Award 2015 (New York).